Promoting Positive Behaviour
in the Early Years

Promoting Positive Behaviour in the Early Years

Karen Morris

Open University Press

Open University Press
McGraw-Hill Education
McGraw-Hill House
Shoppenhangers Road
Maidenhead
Berkshire
England
SL6 2QL

email: enquiries@openup.co.uk
world wide web: www.openup.co.uk

and Two Penn Plaza, New York, NY 10121-2289, USA

First published 2015

A catalogue record of this book is available from the British Library

ISBN-13: 978-0-335-26298-4
ISBN-10: 0-335-26298-8
eISBN: 978-0-335-26299-1

Library of Congress Cataloging-in-Publication Data
CIP data applied for

Typeset by Aptara, Inc.

Fictitious names of companies, products, people, characters and/or data
that may be used herein (in case studies or in examples) are not intended to
represent any real individual, company, product or event.

Printed and bound by CPI Group (UK) Ltd, Croydon, CR0 4YY

Praise for this book

"Karen is a highly respected professional who draws on a wealth of experience working with young children and the adults who support them to produce an accessible and practical book. She gets the balance just right between explaining the theory behind an approach to enable the practitioner to understand why it is important and giving real-life examples to ensure that the reader can put this into practice within their professional context.

Based on sound theory and evidence-based practice, this book draws on approaches such as positive psychology and self-determination theory.

Throughout, the book remains child-centred, concluding with parent and practitioner viewpoints which add depth and detail to the framework provided.

Essential reading for all those working with young children who want to further develop their understanding and skills in nurturing children's development and enabling children to grow and flourish."

Dr Julia Katherine, Inclusion Commissioning Manager,
Portsmouth City Council

"The world is waking-up to the fact that providing <u>quality</u> early childhood education is a key way to raise educational standards and to improve society. At the same time, there is a growing concern with regard to poor behaviour culminating in a statement from Ofsted in 2014 that a vast amount of time in schools is wasted due to, "a culture of casual acceptance" of bad behaviour." Karen Morris begins by shocking us with the statistic that in 2012-2013 there were 1 680 fixed term exclusion issued to children aged 4 years or younger in state funded schools in England during 2012-2013. However, this

is not a negative picture. Karen goes on to draw together theory and practice in a comprehensive and in-depth exploration of the factors that impact young children's development and behaviour. Theories that we are familiar with such as attachment, are given a new dimension when Karen guides us to consider concepts such as deep-rooted relatedness. More recent research included from the field of neuroscience challenges us to consider what impacts children's brain development, behaviour and well-being. We are constantly guided to re-examine what we think we know, always underpinned by a deep understanding of the child's perspective. For example, we may have thought that we knew why key persons are important to children's development, but Karen takes us to new depths of understanding by exploring concepts such as mind-mindedness.

The use of reflection, key points and case studies enable the reader to reflect on the fundamental issues in relation to real children and families. Constructive and helpful strategies suggested throughout the text, give practical ideas to support the development of positive behaviour in young children that can have a life-long impact. The book is positive, challenging and inspirational, successfully meeting its aim to provide approaches that support children's development in ways that meet their emotional need and enable them to delight in their interests and learning. We have been waiting for a book such as this. It is essential reading for early years' professionals and parents, and for anyone interested in promoting positive behaviour and providing the very best for our children."

Professor Pat Preedy, Curtin University (W. Australia)

"Coping with challenging behaviour in an early years setting can be demanding. This text provides an affirmative approach to meeting the needs of children in the early years by using Deci and Ryan's (2000) self-determination theory to outline an original approach to develop practitioners' knowledge, skills and understanding. This book skilfully links theory with practice and makes clear and helpful links to the Early Years Foundation Stage. The case snippets provide excellent examples of situations that are regularly encountered by practitioners. An exploration of parenting styles would be very helpful to parents as well as practitioners. Positive practical suggestions, underpinned by accessible theory, are provided for planning for a child whose behaviour is causing concern. This is a refreshing text that should be available in every early years setting; by reading this practitioners would gain a deep understanding of

the positive approaches to benefit the development of the children in their care."

Julie Wharton, Senior Lecturer at Department for Teacher Development,
Winchester University

"This is a book full of wisdom and practicality. Drawing from both self-determination theory and other state-of-the-art perspectives on motivation and child development, this work will help parents, teachers and anyone caring for children to better help them find the pathways not only to positive adjustment, but to thriving and wellness."

Richard M. Ryan, Professor at Institute for Positive Psychology and
Education, Faculty of Health Sciences, Australian Catholic University

"This is quite simply a lovely book. It takes as its premise a theoretically- and research-informed understanding of how young children's behaviour is formed in context and considers all behaviour development within a positive framework. Its approach is based on fostering the deep-rooted relatedness, competence and autonomy that underpin emotionally healthy behaviour. Theory and research are thoroughly, clearly and digestibly explained, making them accessible to all readers without over-simplification. Boxed tasks and reflection activities ensure that the reader engages fully with the material and relates it to their own experiences, while summaries at the end of chapters provide a clear overview of what has been covered. This is an excellent text for anyone concerned with supporting young children's social and emotional development."

Dr Jane Payler, Senior Lecturer in Education,
The University of Winchester

Contents

List of figures

List of tables

Acknowledgements

My family has always been my greatest support. Particular thanks are due to Tim who behaved impeccably despite the impact writing the book made on our home life.

Penny Lawrence was interested and helpful throughout. The case snippet on Jordan (Chapter 7) was influenced by her work.

Thanks are also due to Cain Richards who helped with the initial literature search as part of the University of Winchester Research Apprenticeship Programme.

1
Introduction

Why write a book about young children's behaviour?

Children's behaviour is often considered newsworthy and such news almost always casts it in a negative light. Some children as young as aged 3 or 4 are being excluded from group settings because adults struggle to cope with their behaviour. UK government statistics indicate that there were 1,680 fixed-term exclusions of children aged 4 and younger from state-funded schools in England in 2012–2013 (DfE 2014a). Behaviour is a topic on which practitioners often say they would welcome more help and training. Compared to other countries (Australia, Canada and the USA), the UK has the widest gap between disadvantaged children and others at school entry with regards to behavioural issues (Bradbury et al. 2012). Furthermore, there is considerable evidence that aggressive behavioural problems tend to 'crystallise' by about age 8 and are much harder to address after that than before (Webster-Stratton and Taylor 2001). Hence understanding, addressing, and ideally preventing, behavioural issues in the early years is of the utmost importance and the focus for this book.

Who is the book for?

This book will support adults who want to promote positive behaviour and well-being in young children. Its main audience is intended to be those who work with children in England; links with the **Early Years Foundation Stage (EYFS)** (DfES 2007; DfE 2012, 2014b) are made throughout the book. However, it may also be useful for parents and a great deal of the research discussed involves parents and children. The book focuses on young children but the principles apply across age ranges and there is much to inform those working with older children whose behaviour is viewed as presenting significant challenges: often the root of such difficulties will lie in the early years. The book shares information about children's development and their needs so that adults can help children to manage their own emotions and behaviour in developmentally appropriate ways. There is no 'quick fix' to solve challenging behaviour. However, when adults begin to adopt a research-informed view of children's development that captures some of the complexities of why children behave in certain ways, they will find that they can generate helpful strategies to move challenging situations forward.

Much of the concern about, and interest in, children's behaviour relates to aggressive and anti-social behaviour, often termed **externalising behaviour**. Of equal importance in this book are **internalised behaviour difficulties**, shown by children who are seriously withdrawn and anxious. The book is relevant for an understanding of both these types of behaviour but in a framework that sees these extremes of behaviour as deriving from the same processes as all behaviour, and responsive to the same approaches as less extreme behaviour. The stance in this book is that behaviour (both norms and extremes) can best be understood using a framework that considers children's needs and what might be appropriate expectations of them, drawing on knowledge of how behaviour develops.

This chapter introduces some of the key concepts underpinning the approach to behaviour taken throughout the book. It is a whistle-stop tour of ideas, planting seeds for the remainder of the book. The ideas will be revisited and explained in greater depth in subsequent chapters.

A positive approach

When professionals ask to see parents about their children's behaviour and when children and young people's behaviour is featured in the media, it is usually unwanted behaviour that is discussed. The implied model of children is often a deficit one. In other words, the underlying assumption is that the problem is located in the child who lacks the desired behaviours. The child and (often) the parents are blamed for the undesired behaviour which is viewed entirely negatively.

In contrast, the approach in this book is a positive one. The emphasis is on finding ways to promote positive behaviour and, where challenging behaviour is evident, to equip those involved to find effective strategies to help the child. Behaviour is seen not as an ingrained and essentially unchangeable aspect of a child but as something that has been, and can be, influenced by many aspects of the environment, including the physical environment, the emotional environment and the reactions of adults and peers.

First, we need to develop a shared understanding of what is meant by 'positive behaviour' (see Task 1.1).

Positive behaviour is not entirely synonymous with what is colloquially referred to as 'good' behaviour, which tends to mean behaviour that makes life easy for adults. A child who is very compliant can be at increased risk of abuse. Behaviour has to be judged in context and taking account of a child's developmental level and experience. The emphasis in this book is on supporting young children in ways that are likely to promote positive behaviour and well-being over the long term. It is accepted that young children need to learn how to behave acceptably and may be clumsy in their attempts to do so. They may also deliberately test the boundaries of what is acceptable. The early years are a

Task 1.1: Consider whether the following examples constitute 'positive' behaviour

- 1-month-old baby Noah frets and cries.
- 1-year-old Ella does not protest when taken from her mother by an unfamiliar social worker.
- 20-month-old Olivia does exactly what her mother tells her not to, watching her mother's reaction all the while. When Mum gets annoyed, Olivia wants to be cuddled and soothed by her.
- 3-year-old Jack avoids areas where play can be messy, keeping his hands and clothes clean.
- 4-year-old Zachary says: 'No, I don't want to!' when his parent suggests he kiss goodbye and hug a distant relative whom he has not met before.
- 5-year-old Lucas, asked to come inside by the teacher, suggests that he will just finish his game first.

Comments

- Babies need to alert their carers if they are uncomfortable. Crying is their means of doing so. This is a typical and 'healthy' behaviour, therefore can be classified as positive.
- A 1-year-old should be attached and very upset to be taken from a parent by an unfamiliar adult. Ella's behaviour is not positive.
- Olivia is testing the boundaries but wants to maintain a close relationship nevertheless. Her behaviour can be construed as positive and part of learning to accept the boundaries.
- Jack may have picked up fears about getting dirty from adult reactions. His behaviour seems constrained and may not be positive.
- Zachary should be allowed to decide whom he feels comfortable to hug and kiss. His views should be respected. His behaviour can be construed as positive.
- Lucas is an immature negotiator. Learning to negotiate is positive. He now needs to learn to distinguish between contexts where negotiation works and those where it is less appropriate.

crucial period for **socialisation**, for **internalisation** of society's expectations. A baby develops from responding to the immediate environment to having **internal representations** or **internal working models** that influence behaviour. How children are helped to internalise their place and role in society has significant effects on their behaviour and well-being. Promoting healthy internalisation – internal working models of the world as essentially a nurturing and exciting place – is a major theme in the book.

A positive approach includes fostering children's skills and strengths, intervening only when appropriate and using alternatives to punishment. This is not to say that a positive approach is a laissez-faire approach or an easy option. The opposite is true at many stages of development. Adults need to be actively and sensitively involved with children if those children are to thrive and develop the deep-rooted relatedness, competence and autonomy that underpin emotionally healthy behaviour. There are, however, at least two major advantages to the types of approaches advocated in this book. One is that though they require time and attention, they foster relationships that are themselves rewarding and tend to balance interactions in the direction of fun and enjoyment. The other is that the time and attention bestowed at crucial periods is an investment that yields huge dividends in terms of positive behaviour for the future.

There is a relatively recent movement in psychology called Positive Psychology (Seligman 2011). The term has a specific meaning, going beyond the positive approach already outlined. Positive Psychology has a scientific basis and is concerned with well-being. Seligman's key contribution is the evidence he provides for the idea that we flourish not by the mere absence of negative psychological states such as depression but by the active cultivation of positive emotions, engagement, meaning, accomplishment and relationships. He stresses that 'there are different skills required for minimising misery and for maximising flourishing' (Seligman 2011:53) . Applying this school of thought to behaviour, the message is that reducing challenging behaviour is also very much about cultivating the positive aspects required for flourishing.

An approach that values children's rights

Adults must exercise their influence over children ethically, thinking about the child's interests as well as the interests of others. Everyone working with children should be aware of the United Nations Convention on the Rights of the Child (UNICEF 1989). This requires that primary consideration is given to children's best interests in all matters affecting them. Children should, of course, be helped and encouraged to develop age-appropriate **prosocial** behaviours such as sharing, waiting for their turn and requesting and receiving in a polite manner. They should not, however, be taught always to comply with adult demands and never to question them. This behavioural expectation, at one time common in British society, greatly increases a child's susceptibility to abuse. Another consideration is that adults should not try and change a child's behaviour simply because they happen to find the behaviour irritating. The question needs to be asked whether it is in the child's interests to be helped to modify the behaviour. Often it will be, as the behaviour may irritate many people and create a barrier to the child's acceptance in many social groups. At other times, the behaviour may not be to the adult's liking but it may cause no harm and serve a useful purpose for the child (for example, 'fidgeting' may help some children maintain concentration).

An approach that acknowledges 'nature' but emphasises nurture

People used to argue about whether criminals are 'born or bred', a form of the old nature versus nurture debate which we now believe to be unhelpfully simplistic. Supported by emerging knowledge of brain maturation, we now view development and behavioural outcomes as involving the interaction of children's biological or genetic inheritance with the environment in which they are raised. The forms of the interaction are not yet fully understood but molecular genetics is beginning to give some glimpses into the complexity and extent of the interactions (Dweck 2013). Whereas it has been customary to view certain genes and temperaments as risk factors for developing behaviour (and other) problems, an emerging and more positive school of thought – known as **differential susceptibility** – provides some evidence that the very children likely to develop behaviour problems when their psychological needs are inadequately met, may thrive to an even greater extent than others in optimal environments (Belsky et al. 2007).

Biology is a part of the picture, though often not the most important part. There are in-built biological predispositions and it is useful to adopt the ideas of evolutionary psychology which assume that there was, historically, a survival advantage to our current genetic structure. An example is that our range of emotions can be understood in this way, with many of the strong 'negative' emotions such as fear, anger and jealousy alerting our ancestors to threats that it was imperative that they avoid or deal with effectively and quickly. The genes for these strong emotions were favoured by natural selection because those who did not receive and heed such signals would not have survived to pass on their genes. These emotions are sometimes seen as troublesome for many youngsters today and this is one of the biological aspects of behaviour explored later in the book.

We are gradually learning just how sophisticated development is and how the expression of genes depends on a wide variety of environmental influences. Human babies are born with more brain development to complete, and with a longer period of dependency on parents, than any other animal. The extent of the development of the brain after birth means that humans are uniquely placed for development to proceed through interaction and in a way that hones their skills and capabilities to match with the requirements of their particular culture and place in the world.

It should be acknowledged that most children's behaviour is not a serious cause for concern and that most parents and most people working with children are promoting positive behaviour perfectly adequately most of the time. As Gopnik et al. (2001: 201) state, 'Nature has designed us to teach babies, as much as it has designed babies to learn'. This book is intended to make parents and practitioners more aware of the science behind what many are already doing and to provide some understanding of where things might go, or have gone, wrong occasionally. Just as man lived in harmony with nature for so long but is now in danger of ruining the planet, so too may modern life have impacted adversely on some aspects of bringing up children.

An approach informed by theory and research

This book is written primarily for those working with children and engaging in study to inform their work. The book has a practical emphasis and its aim is to help readers use theory to devise effective strategies to help children. A **theory** is a set of ideas which describe, explain and, ideally, allow prediction of behaviour. The theories chosen for discussion in this book have been selected as being useful in illuminating behaviour and, crucially, for generating possible ways of moving situations forward in a constructive fashion. Behaviour is complex and there will be severe limitations to any approach based solely on handy hints or top tips because these can never take full account of the many different reasons that might underlie superficially similar behaviour. A child who has been severely emotionally neglected and a child with autistic spectrum differences may both avoid eye contact and shun adult interaction but the causes of their behaviour – and the approaches for helping them – are very different. By exploring in some depth the understandings about behaviour derived from theory, readers will be in a strong position to devise strategies and adapt them in a meaningful way to promote positive behaviour in their own work contexts.

Sociocultural and **humanist** perspectives feature strongly throughout the book. Vygotsky is the father of sociocultural ideas which stress the 'nurture' side of nature/nurture interaction. Vygotsky began to formulate his ideas as early as the 1920s, long before current understandings of infant brain development, but nevertheless his ideas sit well with current knowledge and draw attention to the crucial importance of context. Vygotsky argued not only that children's development takes place in a sociocultural context but that the sociocultural context determines *what* is developed. When we travel, we often become particularly aware that different cultures produce and value different types of behaviour. On a family trip to Japan, we were struck by how deferential people were and made efforts to be more deferential in our own behaviour, bowing and lowering our eyes. There were, however, many social niceties that we were not attuned to and despite our efforts, our behaviour as well as our appearance, clearly marked us out as foreigners.

Two major implications of sociocultural ideas regarding development should be flagged up here. The first is that, to a large extent, the behaviour we see in children is the behaviour cultivated by their circumstances. A view of behaviour as acquired through learning is essentially positive as it implies that change is possible. A second implication is that we need to be aware that the predominant ideas in a society about children's behaviour will usually be those of the influential sections of the population. The norms of behaviour expected in British schools and settings tie in closely with white, middle-class norms. It is essential to recognise that many children come from different backgrounds and experiences and that it can be illuminating to consider their behaviour in terms of the sociocultural environments that influence them. Such children include but are not limited to children from ethnic minorities. Children from white, working-class backgrounds can arguably be even more alienated from our education systems and their expectations.

Sociocultural models give adults a strong influence on children's behavioural development. Children receive clear and consistent messages when parents and practitioners work together. The examples these adults set, and their responses to children, are crucial factors in children's environment. The importance of partnership working, and some ideas for addressing the challenges it can raise, form the topic of Part 4 of the book.

Humanist perspectives maintain that people naturally tend towards psychological as well as physical growth and that they seek meaning in their lives. Children do not need to be goaded into action; what they need is structure and guidance, an environment that allows them to realise their potential.

The major theoretical approaches used in the book sit comfortably with the approaches advocated in the EYFS. While the EYFS (DfE 2014b) does not explicitly make reference to theory, much of it is informed by theory and research (for example, David et al. 2003; Evangelou et al. 2009). This book will develop readers' understanding of the theoretical background that underlies some of the EYFS, thus equipping them to promote positive behaviour from an informed position. The non-statutory guidance material that supports the EYFS – *Development Matters* (Early Education supported by DfE 2012) – presents further invaluable guidance for practitioners on what they can do and provide to support children's development. There are strong connections between the approaches advocated here and the advice in *Development Matters*. The book will enable readers to understand the rationale behind the guidance and thus to implement it with insight and appropriate flexibility for differing needs.

Research comes in many different forms. Often researchers report **correlations**. A correlation between two factors means that there appears to be a relationship between them. It does not necessarily mean that one factor causes the other (see Box 1.1). Often we are inclined to interpret a correlation in a causal fashion because it seems to make sense, but this is bad science. A much stronger case for cause and effect can be established by **experimental** work or by **longitudinal** studies.

Box 1.1: Correlations: interpret with care!

Jogulekar (2012) notes that the chocolate consumption of countries correlates with the number of Nobel Prizes they have won. We are unlikely to believe that eating more chocolate will win us more Nobel Prizes (or that winning more Nobel Prizes increases our consumption of chocolate).

There have been serious cases of correlations being mistakenly interpreted as causal. Before it was established that Down syndrome results from a chromosomal difference, a study found a correlation between electric shock in pregnancy and Down syndrome. This led to the suggestion that electric shock caused Down syndrome. This was probably very

(Continued)

upsetting for parents of a Down syndrome child. How did the correlation arise? It is possible that it was a pure fluke. Another possibility is that, asked if they had had an electric shock in pregnancy, mothers of Down syndrome, searching for an explanation of their child's syndrome, remembered or even thought they remembered, receiving an electric shock. Other mothers would not have 'raked over' their memories of the pregnancy searching for explanation of things not proceeding as they hoped. They may well have forgotten any electric shocks suffered.

The next time you read of a correlation and are tempted to assume a causal relationship between factors, think 'chocolate and Nobel Prize', 'electric shock and Down syndrome' and pause before jumping to conclusions.

In a well-designed experiment, variables are manipulated systematically and there is a control group matched to the experimental group on everything but the variable (intervention) of interest. Experiments can provide the most convincing evidence of cause and effect. However, there are ethical limitations on the experiments that can be carried out on children. There may also be questions over the degree to which effects captured in the artificial laboratory situation are representative of effects at work in real life. **Naturalistic** studies, in contrast, involve observation of children in their natural contexts, such as the family or an education and care setting.

Longitudinal studies follow children over time. Rather than just noting a correlation at one point in time and suggesting a causal relationship, they continue to monitor development over time. The idea that, for example, the extent to which parents talk about negative emotions affects their children's ability to empathise with others would be considerably strengthened if it was shown that parents who spoke about negative emotions to their children at time A had children who showed more evidence of empathy at times B and C. The conclusions of naturalistic studies are considerably strengthened if they are longitudinal in design.

This book aims to give information that is based as much as possible on high quality research that elucidates cause and effect. Where possible, conclusions are backed by experimental or longitudinal naturalistic studies. It is recognised, however, that while a scientific approach has yielded significant advances in understanding behaviour, much is still to be learned. When trying to work effectively to help children with behavioural problems, we need to be tentative and form a **hypothesis** (an informed, best guess) about what might be happening. The hypothesis guides action to try to solve the problem. An initial hypothesis may turn out to be wrong, sometimes it is necessary to revise the hypothesis and try again.

Returning to the issue of correlation, there are many statistics about behaviour difficulties. Correlations between poverty and behavioural problems are repeatedly reported (for example, Allen 2011). In the opening paragraph of the chapter it was noted that the UK has a wider gap between disadvantaged children and others at school entry with regards to behavioural issues than Australia, Canada and the USA (Bradbury et al. 2012). These statistics do not reveal why poverty and disadvantage are associated with behavioural difficulties. Such statistics can be very useful as a broad guide to how to best allocate scarce resources to the neediest. They should not be used to stereotype or form negative expectations of large sections of our communities. The approach taken in this book is one of considering any child and family individually where there is concern about behaviour.

An approach based on needs

A well-known formulation of needs is offered by Maslow's (1943) hierarchy of needs. Maslow felt that basic needs such as the need for food and shelter had to be met in order for people to be able to move on to satisfying needs further up the hierarchy. Only when the physiological, safety, social and esteem needs were met could people meet their highest level needs, which he termed the need for 'self-actualisation'.

The hierarchy of needs is useful for thinking about children's unmet needs. Readers will see links to it in the content of later chapters. Maslow's hierarchy has intuitive appeal to many working with children. We understand that hungry children (or adults) struggle to concentrate on demanding activities and that those (children or adults) going through emotional upheaval at home may similarly struggle to apply themselves. We should also, however, as noted by Hooper (2012: 21), recognise the powerful drives towards exploration (learning), love and aspirational goals that achieve expression in many people whose basic physical and safety needs are far from fully met. Of course, trying to ensure that children's basic physical and safety needs are met is the first duty on all those working with children. Nevertheless, we may do children a disservice if we do not acknowledge and provide opportunities for all their needs, alongside trying to address any shortcomings in the provision for their basic needs.

The model of needs used in this book is less well-known but it is simple and powerful in helping us understand and support positive behaviour. It comes from the work of two American psychologists, Edward Deci and Richard Ryan, who developed **self-determination** theory, a theory of human motivation (Deci and Ryan 2000, 2002). The theory has made a huge impact in many spheres, ranging from workplace motivation to increasing the effectiveness of public health campaigns and from environmental issues to education (Deci and Ryan 2002). Self-determined behaviour is behaviour that a person has freely chosen and feels comfortable with. Behaviour that is impulsive and regretted later would not be considered self-determined. Nor would behaviour that derives primarily from others' expectations – be they parents, teachers or peers. Self-determined behaviour results from 'healthy' internalisation of societal demands.

Self-determination theory posits three innate psychological needs that people (not just children) are striving to meet. These are the needs for relatedness, autonomy and competence (Figure 1.1). Put simply, people thrive and have a sense of well-being when in an environment or situation that enables the three key needs for relatedness, autonomy and competence to be met. If someone is thwarted in having any or all of these needs met, there will be a psychological cost, often displayed in behaviour, which may take the form of anxiety, lack of empathy, aggression or myriad other forms. In this model, much unwanted behaviour is interpreted in terms of people compensating or developing defences to cope with the thwarting of their needs for relatedness, autonomy and competence. The model will be further explained and used to illuminate behaviour and to generate positive approaches throughout the book. The model raises the following key question in terms of promoting positive behaviour: what can be done to further help the child meet their needs for relatedness, competence and autonomy?

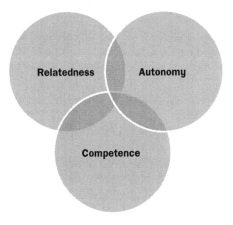

Figure 1.1 The three psychological needs
Source: Based on Deci and Ryan (2000).

Reflection 1.1: What do the terms relatedness, autonomy and competence mean to you?

- Think of some examples of how your own needs in these three spheres are satisfied.
- Does your work enable satisfaction of these needs?

Where did self-determination theory come from?

Deci and Ryan did not just dream up self-determination theory. They were involved in experimental work on motivation for many years. Later (in Chapter 7) we will look at some experimental findings on the effects of rewards on motivation which challenged existing models. Over time, Deci and Ryan developed their own model that was consistent with experimental findings and, furthermore, generated predictions that have subsequently been confirmed by experiments. Thus, there is **empirical** evidence for their model and it has predictive power. This makes it a strong and useful model with applications in many spheres, including promoting positive behaviour. In addition, the model has at its core the humanist beliefs that people actively try to make sense of the world and create meaning in their lives. Its ideas fit comfortably with the values of most people who choose to work with children and they are entirely consistent with the principles of a unique child, the importance of positive relationships and enabling environments, principles which underpin the EYFS (DfE 2014b). The use of the model in this book keeps the focus away from any medical diagnosis of children whose behaviour is of concern, instead maintaining a focus on strategies that might be helpful.

Application of the model in this book

Self-determination theory (Deci and Ryan 2000) is a lifespan model. The three psychological needs are considered to be universal and relevant for all age groups. In this book the model is applied not only to children but also to the adults living or working with the children – their parents, carers, teachers and others. When considering how well a setting promotes positive behaviour, it is fruitful to consider the extent to which it provides for the three psychological needs of children and also those of parents and practitioners (the term 'parents' in this book denotes anyone with parental responsibility for a child). When looking in depth at the behaviour of a particular child, an effective programme will look at how the needs of all involved are being met – often this is a triangle of child, parent(s) and practitioner(s). The majority of the book is devoted to developing understanding of evidence-based ways of promoting positive behaviour in children, but Part 4 is crucial and focuses on some of the dynamics of working in partnership, including the needs of parents and practitioners.

The book explores some of what is known about the developmental expression of the needs for relatedness, competence and autonomy and the contexts that enable children to flourish. A baby and a pre-schooler both have a need to feel competent, but the expression of competence is different as development proceeds. Babies are entirely dependent on others for care – how then does the need for autonomy fit into the picture? We know that children need structure, support and guidance as they develop. How are these to be provided in a balanced way that also allows satisfaction of a need for autonomy? In self-determination theory, the type of support children receive as they develop, the nature of the socialisation processes, are crucial. As we will explore further in subsequent chapters, environmental factors (in the broadest sense and including adult behaviour) influence how children internalise the demands that arise as they grow to take their place in their family, childcare and education settings and other communities. The form of this internalisation of 'societal' demands has a major effect on children's well-being and behaviour. It influences whether they feel in control and responsible for their own actions (self-determined) or controlled by others.

Research illuminating the developmental processes alerts us to (or reminds us) what to expect in children's development. Without being aware of the usual pattern of development, we may construe a child's behaviour as a concern when it is entirely in line with the range of typical development. Most people take a toddler's tantrums in their stride; similar behaviour from a 10-year-old is likely to raise eyebrows. With knowledge of the processes of development, the possible manifestations of unmet needs can be recognised and plans devised to try to address the root causes of what presents as challenging or concerning behaviour. The material to be covered highlights some useful progress that has been made in understanding children's social and emotional development. In so doing, it enables readers to bring knowledge to bear on their interpretations of children's behaviour, and to adopt a positive, constructive approach to trying to help.

The bodies of research we are going to draw on often pre-date Deci and Ryan's (2000) self-determination theory. Many use different vocabulary and concepts from Deci and Ryan but nevertheless there are links to be made and the aim here is to do so. Some use broad constructs (such as 'attachment style' or 'parenting style') that capture an array of elements; others have a much more specific focus (such as type of praise or executive function). There is overlap in some of the constructs discussed but different research foci add their own dimensions to our understanding. Practitioners are accustomed to hearing that child development is holistic since this is language used in the EYFS (DfE 2014b). Strands of development are interrelated. Social development and emotional development are not completely separate from cognitive development, nor, for example, is understanding of emotions completely separate from interacting with peers. It is also important to note that the three areas of need in self-determination theory (relatedness, competence and autonomy) overlap (see Figure 1.1) – they influence one another in ways that will become clear through the book. Any attempt to map disparate bodies of research onto a single model requires a 'best fit' approach. This 'best fit' approach is felt to be justified by the value of self-determination theory in providing a framework for illuminating positive approaches to behaviour.

The structure of the book

The book is divided into four parts, three of which relate to the three psychological needs: relatedness, autonomy and competence. Each need is introduced in general terms, in a way that captures the lifespan context and encourages readers to think about its applicability to themselves as adults, whether as parents or professionals working with children. Next, each of these parts focuses on children and 'unpacks' the need by considering landmark research relating to the developmental expression of that need and what adults can do or provide to promote need fulfilment.

Part 4 considers partnership working including meeting the psychological needs of parents and practitioners when working to promote children's positive behaviour.

Key points

- Positive behaviour is promoted by providing environments that enable people to meet their psychological needs.
- Positive behaviour does not just mean complying easily with adults.
- Nurture is usually more important than nature in the genesis of problem behaviour. Much behaviour is learned or shaped by circumstances.
- Theory can provide constructive ways of viewing behaviour and generating strategies to support positive behaviour.
- Correlations between factors should be treated with care as they do not necessarily mean that one factor has caused the other. Understanding cause and effect is important when devising effective strategies. Experiments and longitudinal studies are to be favoured when trying to establish cause and effect.
- As they grow, children internalise the behavioural expectations of their communities. The way in which this internalisation takes place has long-term consequences for their behaviour and well-being.
- Self-determination theory, as developed by Deci and Ryan (2000), posits that environments that support the needs for relatedness, autonomy and competence will promote healthy internalisation and positive behaviour.

Part 1
Relatedness

'I belong'

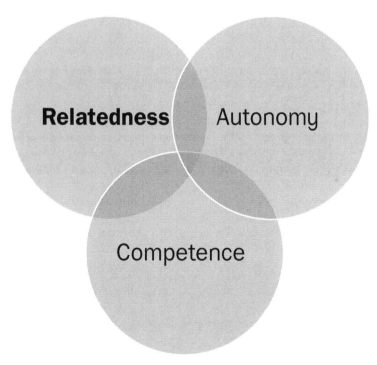

Figure P1.1 The three psychological needs: focus on relatedness
Source: Based on Deci and Ryan (2000).

Introduction to Part 1

Relatedness is a universal and lifelong need. We all recognise the fundamental role of relationships – be they family, friends or romantic partners – in most people's lives. There is evidence of physical as well as psychological health benefits when we have supportive relationships in our lives (Berkman and Glass 2000). Babies and young children are dependent on adults. Relationships influence whether young children survive but, more than this, whether they thrive.

Before turning to how relatedness develops between young children and those caring for them, it may be useful to take a broader look at relatedness, from the readers' perspectives as adults. What does the healthy expression of relatedness between people look like? Which factors promote the healthy expression and which factors lead to a less healthy expression of the same need? Consider the bullet points below which summarise the view of relatedness as portrayed in Deci and Ryan's (2000) self-determination theory. Developing a clear view of healthy adult relatedness can provide a valuable context for considering relatedness between children and adults. The nature of the relationships is different and must be so, to take account of children's developmental needs. However, understanding what healthy relatedness is – and what it is not – can highlight the possible long-term effects of some ways of interacting with babies and children.

Related individuals:

- Feel unconditionally loved and cared for and love and care for others unconditionally.
- Depend on important others.
- Have a sense of security and of mattering.
- Feel linked to the values of their main social groups, being influenced by them and influencing them.
- Consider others without compromising their sense of self.
- Value co-operation and collaboration.

Relatedness is not:

- Total dependence on someone else (after infancy).
- Always being part of a group and avoiding solitary activities.

- Feeling unable to express opinions that challenge the group.
- Never competing against one of the group.

Environments that support relatedness

- Accord equal value to each person and value people in the round for their unique qualities and not simply for their achievements.
- Provide both time and space for people to be together when they wish.
- Highlight shared goals, developed together.
- Promote co-operation and collaboration.
- Recognise that airing of differences and resolving them can be healthy. There may be better ways of doing things.
- Encourage mutual supportiveness including knowledge of each other's aspirations and empathy when obstacles are encountered.

Environments that undermine relatedness: cold

- Value some people more than others and accord value on the basis of particular characteristics/skills/achievements.
- Have no times when task focus is relaxed and no places where people can share 'down time'.
- Impose goals.
- Are competitive with individuals pitted against each other.
- Discourage articulation and discussion of views that might challenge established goals/practice.
- Ignore people's aspirations and the challenges they face.

Environments that undermine relatedness: no room to breathe

- Make it clear that you are part of a select group valued for particular characteristics/behaviours/skills.
- Demand a lot of time spent with others and not task-focused.
- Assume unquestioning support of group goals.
- Everything has to be done together.
- 'We think and breathe as one'.
- No privacy – we share every facet of your life.

Reflection P1.1: Feelings of relatedness

Reflect on the definition of relatedness given above. Consider to what degree you feel 'related'. This may vary in different contexts and your feelings of relatedness are likely to have varied at different times in your life. To what extent have you experienced relatedness-supporting or relatedness-undermining environments? Reflect with regard to the following:

- the home you grew up in;
- your education;
- your current living arrangements;
- your workplace.

Relatedness in the early years

Early experiences of relatedness set such a strong template for future relationships and have such a powerful influence on our lives, mental well-being and behaviour that the type of attachment bond a parent-to-be will form with their yet-to-be-born baby can be predicted with 75 per cent accuracy from the answers given to the questions in the Adult Attachment Inventory (AAI) (Main 1996).

Developing secure attachment (relatedness) in infancy is significantly associated with positive well-being and behaviour. Relatedness is important across the lifespan and across contexts. Positive relationships are not only a source of pleasure and support but they exert a positive influence on how we perceive and react to events. A practitioner might make exactly the same comment to two children about where they can ride the bikes. Depending on their personal attachment history and their relationship with the practitioner, one child may interpret this as helpful information and cycle only where indicated. The other child may interpret the comment as controlling and fight against such control by cycling in the forbidden area.

Positive relationships make it easier to promote positive behaviour and to recover after disputes. When parents have formed secure relationships with their children, the children will feel comfortable enough to explore behavioural limits but they will also want to maintain the warm relationship. The relationship makes behaviour management both easier and more rewarding. In settings too, the warmth of relationships is key. Singer and de Haan (2007) observed and analysed the conflicts of many young children in settings. The children found it easier to compromise and negotiate within friendships, or with adults with whom they have a close relationship. The quality of relationships affects the quality of interaction and learning. Shared imaginary play – a particularly important source of learning for young children (Part 3) – occurs most often within close and affectionate friendships (Cutting and Dunn 2006). Sibling relationships differ in quality and it is this that determines whether they promote positive behaviour and learning. Within an affectionate sibling relationship, a younger sibling often develops advanced play skills and social and emotional understanding.

This section on relatedness concentrates on attachment theory because of the strong evidence of the impact of early attachment on behaviour.

Structure of Part 1

- Chapter 2 – 'The value of a secure attachment bond: "I need to feel safe, special and valued"'. This chapter explores the origins of attachment theory and both the immediate and long-term benefits of secure attachment. It looks at how parents and those working with children can promote secure attachment through sensitive, responsive care.

- Chapter 3 – 'Understanding insecure attachments and ways to help: "Understand that this behaviour started as self-protection"'. This chapter develops understanding of the different ways that children try to meet their need for relatedness in less than ideal circumstances and the impact on their well-being and behaviour. It helps adults to recognise these patterns and discusses ways to help those at risk of insecure attachments.

Relatedness and the EYFS

Relatedness is a major theme running right through the EYFS (DfE 2014b) as illustrated in Box P1.1.

Box P1.1: Relatedness and the EYFS

- One of the four overarching principles is that 'children learn to be strong and independent through positive relationships'.
- The Key Person requirement derives from attachment theory. It states that:

   Each child must be assigned a key person. Their role is to help ensure that every child's care is tailored to meet their individual needs..., to help the child become familiar with the setting, offer a settled relationship for the child and build a relationship with their parents.

   (DfE 2014b)

- The designation of personal, social and emotional development (PSE) as a prime area of learning and development emphasises its importance. PSE includes positive relationships.

Source: (DfE 2014b).

2

The value of a secure attachment bond

'I need to feel safe, special and valued'

If you want children who thrive in all respects, including displaying positive behaviour, the best single piece of advice is to provide babies and young children with consistent, responsive caregiving. This means caregiving that is delivered by one or a consistent small group of adults, with the adults being attuned to the baby or child, picking up on the range of cues the child offers – subtle cues that the baby is interested and would like to interact, or is tired and would prefer to rest (Sroufe 1990) as well as the more obvious cues such as crying. Such caregiving enables babies to form and maintain a secure **attachment bond** with the caregivers. By dint of being soothed and having their needs met by their caregivers, the scene is set for two very important developments. First, babies who are soothed and comforted learn over time to stabilise (regulate) their own emotions. Emotional regulation is important for positive behaviour. Second, when babies and children are responded to in a way that meets not just their physical needs but recognises their individuality, their likes and dislikes, the times when they want to interact and play, their emerging sense of humour and their idiosyncrasies, then they develop the sense that they matter, that they are special and valued. This too is important for behaviour. Children who are supported in understanding and valuing themselves develop a clear yet positive sense of self, which is a foundation for autonomy. They also tend to understand and value others too. Early relationships form the template for future relationships. The child who feels secure and valued has a tremendous foundation for the joys and challenges of relationships throughout life. Such a child is much more likely to be happy, to give and receive appropriate care, to take others' feelings into account and generally to behave positively than is a child with less fortunate early experiences. These secure foundations produce a dizzying array of benefits (Figure 2.1).

Some bold and sweeping claims have been made in the paragraph above. They are the claims of modern attachment theory, 'perhaps the most widely-used and influential explanatory framework in psychology' (Meins 2014). In order to apply these ideas to benefit children and families, it is important to understand attachment theory in some depth (see Box 2.1). Attachment theory has had a major influence on the EYFS (DfE 2014b) and has informed the **Key Person**

Figure 2.1 Some of the 'dizzying array of later outcomes' associated with secure attachment
Source: Based on Thompson (2013).

requirement. While some practitioners think of this role in terms of tasks to be performed, especially records to be kept, it is really about forming a close relationship with a child.

Box 2.1: John Bowlby (1907–1990): father of attachment theory

John Bowlby was a British psychiatrist who practised as a clinician and led a research team at the Tavistock Clinic in London. He developed the theory that children are biologically predisposed to form an affectional bond or attachment to their mothers and that the quality of this bond is the key to lifelong psychological health (Bowlby 2005).

Key influences
- *Personal experience*. Bowlby saw relatively little of his own mother during infancy, being raised at a time and within a social class where most of the childcare was delegated to nannies. He was very fond of his nanny, Minnie, and devastated when she suddenly left and he received no explanation why (Bowlby 2005: xi).
- *His work with 'maladjusted' boys*. Bowlby noted that some were 'clingy', staying near him as much as possible. Others were remote

(Continued)

and avoided contact. Many had histories of disrupted mothering (Bretherton 1992). The theory Bowlby developed could explain these differing reactions in terms of attachment experiences.

- *Reaction against Freud's psychosexual theory.* This was the dominant tradition at the time, with its emphasis on psychic conflict, much of it to do with unconscious fantasy. Bowlby came to believe that real events, rather than unconscious fantasies, were at the root of psychological development.
- *Ethology, the study of animal behaviour* under natural circumstances and viewing it from an evolutionary stance. The ethologist Konrad Lorenz famously demonstrated that greylag geese imprint on (learn about and follow) the first moving thing they see. There is a critical period of 13–16 hours after hatching for imprinting. Usually geese imprint on their mother but there are famous pictures of geese which imprinted on Lorenz as he was the first moving thing they saw in the critical period.

Note: Bowlby has been criticised for his emphasis on the mother as the primary attachment figure. Modern attachment theory is much less gendered.

Attachment theory: key concepts

Attachment theory holds that the bonds formed between babies and carers are about much more than ensuring that the babies receive the physical care they need. Secure attachment is about providing babies with a bedrock of relatedness that promotes their learning and well-being throughout life. The attachment bond is a specific bond, developed most intensely to one figure (the **primary attachment figure**) but also often to a small group of other individuals (**secondary attachment figures**), with a child showing a clear hierarchy of preference. A newborn is predisposed to form a bond. It is the environment (the emotional environment, the reaction of adult(s) to the child) that determines the quality of the attachment that takes place. The affectional bond between attachment figure and child strengthens as the infant develops and (hopefully) receives sensitive, responsive care from an attuned attachment figure (Table 2.1).

The bond will be secure if the carer not only reliably meets the infant's physical needs and but also picks up on all a baby's cues and enjoys the infant's company. The bond is emotionally charged, bringing predominately joy and delight to both in securely bonded pairs but with more emphasis on distress and frustration in less securely attached relationships. The bond forms in early babyhood and usually persists throughout life. While the bond, once formed, exists all the time, the attachment behaviours that evidence the bond (behaviours such as searching, crying and clinging, designed to bring or keep infant and attachment

Table 2.1 Typical development of attachment behaviours

Development stage	Attachment behaviour
0–3 months	I'm usually relatively happy to be passed from one doting carer to another
3–6 months	I prefer Mummy or other very familiar people to look after me
From 7 months	I try to stay near Mummy. If I can, I'll crawl around after her. I'll watch her closely and I love interacting with her. If she goes away, I often wait by the door for her and sometimes I cry
12–18 months	I really let people know now when Mummy is not available – I protest very loudly!
By 48 months	Now I completely understand that Mummy will come back soon and that she cares about me even when she is not with me for a little while. Usually I'm fine but I want her badly when I'm ill or upset

Note: the strongest attachment need not necessarily be to the mother but often is.

figure close) are only evident at times and particularly when threat is perceived. States such as hunger or tiredness can increase attachment behaviours, as can 'life events' such as the arrival of a sibling or any other change in the emotional dynamics of home. With age, the form of attachment behaviours varies though even in adulthood, trauma often triggers an urgency to contact or be with our parents or other primary attachment figures.

Case snippet 2.1: Jacob

Jacob, 6 months old, has been unsettled all afternoon. Shula, his Key Person, feeds him, changes him and tries to distract him with mobiles and rattles but he continues to cry. The manager comes in and sees that Shula may have to leave Jacob to tend to the other children in her care. The manager considers taking Jacob to soothe him but instead offers to look after Shula's other children and tells Shula not to worry about them, to concentrate on Jacob. Shula takes Jacob over to the rocking chair in the quiet area and sits with him. She realises how tense she is and makes a conscious effort to breathe more slowly and deeply and to be very gentle holding Jacob and rocking the chair. The manager pops over and puts some soothing music on. Slowly Jacob (and Shula) become calmer. Jacob eventually drifts into a light sleep but his eyelids flicker when Shula stops rocking so she just sits and rocks.

From their attachment experiences with their primary attachment figure, children build up an internal working model, a mental representation of themselves in relation to others that influences later relationships. Throughout this book it is stressed that the way in which people internalise or mentally represent their understanding of the world has major implications for well-being and behaviour. The fortunate child with secure early attachment develops an internal working model which views the self as worthy of love and others as trustworthy. Such a child is likely to replicate an appropriate balance of relatedness and autonomy in future close relationships and so to thrive, unencumbered by psychological and concomitant behaviour issues.

Bowlby (1966: 59) famously stated: '[M]aternal care in infancy and early childhood is essential for mental health. This is a discovery comparable in magnitude to that of the role of vitamins in physical health.' This was a revolutionary view at a time when keeping babies alive and healthy was regarded as the key aspiration. Attachment theory implied that, important as physical health is, it is not enough. The theory challenged some childcare practices deriving mainly from health concerns, such as limiting handling of babies to protect them from germs and removing sick children from their parents for long periods of time to convalesce in healthy locations. Mary Ainsworth (Ainsworth and Marvin 1995) summarised the implications of her research by saying, 'Never miss an opportunity to hold a baby'. Such advice not only contradicted that of health professionals but also opposed that of behavioural psychologists. **Behavioural learning theory** implied that picking up crying babies would reinforce (reward) crying behaviour and increase its likelihood. This fitted in with popular ideas that 'pandering to' babies would 'spoil' them. Ainsworth's observational data following families over time presented a different story (see Box 2.2).

Box 2.2: Mary Ainsworth (1913–1999): pioneer in developing attachment theory through scientific methods

Mary Ainsworth, an American Canadian, had researched 'security theory' (Blatz 1940, cited in Bretherton 1992) at the University of Toronto before coming to London and briefly joining Bowlby's research team at the Tavistock Clinic. She then travelled and researched in Uganda before settling in the United States.

Mary Ainsworth's methods bestowed scientific credibility on attachment theory by providing evidence. Her findings also shaped the direction of the theory.

- She carried out painstaking naturalistic observations in both Uganda and the United States (Baltimore, Maryland). In the Ugandan study (1953–1955) she regularly visited 26 infant–mother pairs, observing them for two hours every fortnight, for up to nine months. In the Baltimore project, she again worked with 26 families, this time recruiting them before the birth of the baby and making 18 visits, each of four hours, during the baby's first year. Ainsworth made detailed observations, recording events in context and noting mothers' comments on their babies as well as their actions towards them. She gathered rich data that yielded insights into the natural development of infant–mother interactions in two very different parts of the world. She recognised that all mother–baby pairs formed bonds but that there were qualitative differences in the nature of the bonds.

- She famously devised an **experimental paradigm** called the '**strange situation**' which is a telling snapshot that seems to capture qualities of the bond developed between babies and their mothers over the first year of life. The design of the 'strange situation' and Ainsworth's interpretations of the findings were informed by her extensive observational 'fieldwork' which, to her, was the most significant part of her work.

The detailed naturalistic studies showed that secure attachment, the type of attachment believed to be healthiest for children's development, emerged when mothers had been sensitive to their baby's signals from birth. Large amounts of close bodily contact, mutual enjoyment of feeding and the mother's ability to comment on the tiny details of her baby's reactions were all associated with secure attachment. Where babies and mothers had enjoyed this close, sensitive, attuned relationship in the early months, the babies were generally content at the end of the first year. Babies who had been held and successfully soothed frequently in the first months sought less contact with their mother at the end of the first year but the contact that took place was warm and both took pleasure in it (Ainsworth and Bell 1970). These babies already had the foundations for secure attachment and positive behaviour.

Meins et al. (2012) found that 'mind-mindedness' was the best predictor of secure attachment. '**Mind-minded**' described mothers who accurately 'read' the minds of their 8-month-olds and commented appropriately (for example, 'you want the rattle' to a child looking at a rattle and obviously pleased to have it passed to her , or 'you're hungry' to a child who was then offered milk which was willingly received). Through mothers' mind-mindedness, securely attached children build a positive and predictable internal model of the mother as comforting and themselves as worthy of comfort and attention to their needs and desires. Through the experience of having their feelings and emotions correctly interpreted and regulated by the mother, they learn over time to regulate their own emotions.

Ainsworth herself drew a distinction between warmth and sensitivity, describing warmth as a general characteristic but sensitivity (responsiveness/

'mind-mindedness') as being in tune with the baby, recognising the baby's initiatives and letting the baby set the pace and style of interaction (Ainsworth and Marvin 1995: 11). A warm carer might have positive but similar interactions with all children but one who is 'mind-minded' would be observed to vary the tempo and style of interaction to suit the signals coming from a particular baby.

In talking about responsive and sensitive care, it is important to be aware of the concept of the 'good enough' parent or carer, a term usually ascribed to Winnicott (1965) and capturing the reality that parents and carers do not have to be 100 per cent responsive or mind-minded in order for children to achieve secure attachment. Tronick's (2007) research suggests that even sensitive mothers 'read' their baby's cues correctly first time only in about a third of instances. Misreading cues and then a correcting interpretation are more common than not. With sensitive care, babies learn that miscuing in social relationships is normal and need not be worrying. Baby and carer can persist in expressing themselves to achieve understanding and to ensure babies' needs are met.

Imitation is something that many adults instinctively do with babies. Reddy (2008: 45) describes imitation as a 'psychological door through which one is immediately led into a world of intentional relations with another person'. Parents and practitioners can usefully adopt imitation as a conscious strategy to help them act in tune with a baby.

In a secure relationship, a child develops trust. The attachment figure provides a **secure base** from which a growing child can explore the world. Attunement works both ways. The child is attuned to the attachment figure, picking up subtle cues from the attachment figure about the safety or otherwise of the environment. The way children look to their parents or carers to gauge what they can do is known as **social referencing** (see Box 2.3). The attached toddler acts as though literally attached to the preferred carer by an elastic rein, venturing to the farthest reaches of the elastic's reach when all is well but seeking proximity (closeness) to the attachment figure when there are signals given out that all is not well or when an external threat is perceived. Secure attachment promotes exploration and learning.

Box 2.3: The visual cliff and social referencing

The 'visual cliff' is an illusory cliff. Babies are placed on a flat, stable transparent surface about one metre above the floor. There is a cloth underneath with a chequerboard pattern. Half-way across the surface, the cloth drops to the ground creating the impression of a steep drop or cliff. The transparent surface continues and the baby is quite safe to crawl on the whole surface despite the appearance of the drop.

Sorce et al. (1985) used the visual cliff with 1-year-olds. Previous work had established that babies of this age perceive the drop and stay on the side they perceive as safe. In this experiment, parents were asked to give babies different cues. Some were asked to be reassuring and to smile and indicate to the child that it was fine to venture onto the 'cliff'; others were asked to look anxious and deter children from doing this.

74 per cent of babies went on the cliff when the parent smiled.

No babies entered the cliff when the parent showed fear

'Social referencing' is the term used to describe how people take cues from others for how to behave. Babies were powerfully influenced by signs from their parents that the cliff was safe.

In settings too, children show social referencing. Singer and de Haan (2007) have carried out extensive research in a variety of day-care settings and report how children tend to look towards the teacher when they are not sure about things or need help. They also glance towards the adult periodically in a way that suggests they find it reassuring to check that the teacher is watching over them.

There has been some consideration of gender roles in promoting children's exploration. Richard Bowlby, son of John Bowlby, has questioned whether John Bowlby underestimated fathers' importance in promoting exciting play and exploration in young children. Richard Bowlby (Newland and Coyl 2010) suggested that mothers might take the lead in providing a secure base for children but that their emphasis on safety and calm, controlled activities, though important, might be a little restrictive for the growing, curious infant. He suggested that mothers' approach needs to be leavened by the more exciting rough-and-tumble play, and generally more daring activities of fathers. Many of us can easily picture a doting Dad throwing up and catching a giggling infant or chasing a squealing toddler, while making loud, mock scary noises.

The possible importance of men in satisfying children's needs for a racier, riskier, more exhilarating type of interactive exploration raises questions for many settings catering for young children. There are very few men working with young children.

The role of fathers in children's development has been an important area of research (Lamb 1978; Grossmann et al. 2008; Bretherton 2010). A parallel can be drawn between the move away from the initial emphasis on (female) gender in attachment theory and the way thinking has developed in 'father' research. Initial claims of a crucial role of certain 'father' activities have now been replaced by a **systems approach** that considers the range of support and styles available to children in a particular family (or setting). Fathers' involvement is beneficial for children on many fronts, including positive behaviour (Lamb 2010). Sensitive fathering has been found to have the same key elements as sensitive mothering. Both involve recognising and responding to children's needs; emotionally engaged interaction (sharing fun, frustration and other feelings); and promoting children's exploration, primarily in directions initiated by the child. Sensitive parenting and care are gender-neutral. Children benefit from having both parents involved in their care. A systems approach recognises a range of reasons why this is the case, ranging from the support, emotional and financial, that parents may provide for each other, through to the benefit to the child of having involved caregivers with different interactional styles (Lamb 2010).

For settings, while it would be desirable to have more men, there are also other implications of this research. Children are likely to benefit from different styles of play and exploration. They need carers whose primary style is calm, caring and nurturing. They also benefit from those who tend to be more rambunctious, adventurous and active. Not all practitioners need to adopt the same style, in fact, it might be unhelpful to do so. Be aware of the value of discussing these issues in settings. Individuals feel comfortable with different ranges of behaviour and some feel threatened by the idea of altering their behaviour or of accepting different behaviour in those around them. Many settings recruit people with similar qualities to those already working there. Newcomers model their behaviour on what they observe. The result of these influences may be a staff team that feels very comfortable with one another but that is depriving children of beneficial access to a variety of interaction styles. In the worst cases, children's risk taking and exploration may be limited as a result of the dominance of what is perceived as a caring, nurturing ethos but is so extreme that some children's drive towards the novel and exciting is not being encouraged. An optimal environment includes diverse interpersonal styles to stimulate children's natural exploratory tendencies.

Box 2.4 indicates some of the features of a setting that would indicate it takes attachment seriously.

Box 2.4: Theory into practice

A setting promoting secure attachments ...
- Prioritises staff retention, knowing that a high staff turnover rate jeopardises attachment.
- Has a planned and gradual settling-in process for children, including a visit to the home by staff as well as visits by the child and parent(s) to the setting.

- Listens to parents and children and their concerns – routines, health issues, preferred activities, food, dislikes, fears and idiosyncrasies.
- Learns about the significant people in the family, pets and other factors in the child's life. For non-verbal children, some parents may like to write 'in the voice of the child' to capture what they believe is important in the child's day-to-day life.
- Shares information about the routine before children begin attendance.
- Is welcoming, supportive and non-judgemental in attitude to parents and children.
- Has Key People who take every chance to cuddle their babies, comfort their children and to connect with them through sharing emotional moments, humour and pleasurable moments.
- Realises the importance of transitional objects to help children settle.
- Acknowledges a child's emotions about separation rather than ignoring or denying them.
- Provides information about the Key Person role to parents, explaining why this relationship with the child is important for the child's well-being and no threat to the parent's own relationship with the child.
- Portrays the Key Person role to parents and staff as primarily about relationships.
- Is flexible in Key Person arrangements and can change the allocated person if the child shows a clear preference for another adult.
- Has an arrangement for times when the Key Person is absent, for example, a 'buddy' system where practitioners are paired and the buddies ensure they get to know children and families so they are a familiar face should the Key Person be absent.
- Ensures that children's changing, feeding and care routines are performed with their Key Person.
- Allows time for Key People to get to know their children, prioritising serendipitous opportunities to enjoy each other's company over rigid timetabling.
- Has practitioners who reflect on the importance of touch, speed of their movements, volume, tone and tempo of their speech in creating a comforting ethos.
- Provides seating and spaces where babies can be cuddled and rocked, toddlers and pre-schoolers can enjoy sitting close to an adult, chatting, singing, playing or reading.
- Provides frequent informal opportunities for sharing information between the Key Person and parents.
- Has Key People who engage in 'mind-minded' interactions with children during feeding, hygiene and other routines as well as during play.

(Continued)

- Recognises clinginess as a possible expression of uncertainty/lack of trust and puts the emphasis on building up trust rather than just directly on reducing the clinginess.
- Has Key People who notice children who appear unemotional and self-contained and make an effort to develop closer relationships with them.
- Takes any naturally arising opportunity to encourage parents to be responsive to their children and to share mutually enjoyable activities or 'downtime' together.
- Uses and advocates imitation as a simple but powerful route to engagement with babies and toddlers.
- Signposts parents to helpful non-stigmatising groups/activities, for example, baby massage, toddler groups.

Longitudinal studies of attachment

Support for the importance of the bond between a baby and the primary caregiver comes from longitudinal studies, i.e. studies that rate the quality of infants' attachment and then follow up those same infants when they are adults. There are now a number of such studies and they provide support for the long-term influence of early attachment. One example is the research carried out by Maselko et al. (2011). They had access to data from a study in Providence, Long Island, USA, where psychologists had rated mother–baby interaction when the babies were 8 months old. Thirty-three years later, the researchers were able to trace and administer checklists about emotional functioning to 482 of the people who had been involved in the study as infants. The findings suggested that infants who were involved in warm relationships with their mothers at age 8 months were significantly less likely to suffer emotional distress as adults. The virtuous cycle of secure attachment is shown in Figure 2.2.

Increasing understanding of neurodevelopment

Since Bowlby and Ainsworth formulated the key concepts in attachment theory, technology has contributed hugely to our understanding of brain and nervous system development and the underlying neurochemistry. This is a complicated, fascinating and at times controversial field. Just as Bowlby was a clinician-scientist, developing theory to inform his practice by synthesising ideas from different fields of study, so too have some more recent clinician-scientists attempted to link attachment theory with how the brain develops and works to incorporate attachment into ambitious, holistic theories of human development uniting psychology, biology, anthropology and other disciplines. Key figures are Allan Schore, Daniel Siegel and Sue Gerhardt. While the details of their ideas will probably change and

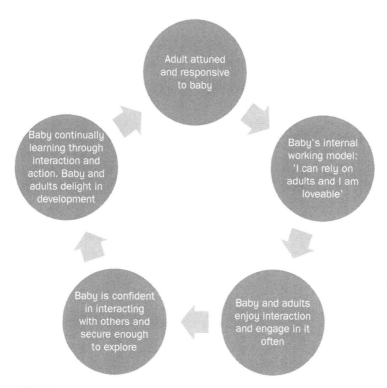

Figure 2.2 Virtuous circle of secure attachment

be refined over time, there are some useful established facts that show support for Bowlby's ideas in terms of neuroscience:

- Babies are born with a strong inclination to be social (this is discussed in Chapter 8).
- The brain has most of its cells (neurons) at birth but many of the connections between them ('the wiring') take place after birth and so are influenced by experience. Interpersonal experiences (relationships) are of particular importance.
- Neurons that fire together wire together. Connections in the brain that are used over and over again will become the strongest connections. Patterns of care are what matter, with a 'mind-minded' pattern promoting secure attachment.
- Connections in the brain increase rapidly but there is a later 'pruning' of connections, retaining the frequently used connections and eliminating those that are rarely used. The timescale for these processes varies for different parts of the brain (Blakemore and Frith 2005). In the visual cortex, there is

a rapid growth of connections at 2–3 months of age, peaking at 8–10 months and then there is pruning of connections until about 10 years of age. By contrast, in the frontal cortex (responsible for many executive functions connected to behaviour, for example, planning, inhibition, emotion control), the rapid growth in connections happens later and the pruning is not complete until early adulthood (Blakemore and Frith 2005: 23).

- The above relates to sensitive periods for aspects of development, i.e. periods when certain pathways within the brain are most easily and strongly established. However, if babies or children are deprived of the normal environmental conditions for development at the usual time, the brain shows an ability to compensate later, though possibly with subtle differences in skills and abilities even in the most successful cases.

Gerhardt (2004) writes very powerfully about the biological basis of attachment and explains how social interaction with carers literally builds the structure (connections) within a baby's brain. She describes the patterns of biochemical reactions that, over time, form a baby's (and later the child's, then the adult's) habitual response. Caring behaviours such as making eye contact, genuine smiling, stroking, taking pleasure in each other's company and being soothed release oxytocin and other 'feel good' chemicals which promote the growth of neural connections and dampen down stress. By contrast, threat, fear and negative emotions release cortisol and other stress hormones which inhibit neural growth and are toxic for well-being if they remain in the body too long. In Gerhardt's explanation of secure attachment, the carer recognises when the baby is upset or frightened and engages in the soothing behaviours which help to stop the release of stress hormones and to dissipate their effects as they are replaced by the 'feel good' chemicals. Babies, who are thus helped to cope with and manage their feelings, learn, over time, to cope more independently. The pattern of being able to maintain a reasonable emotional (and chemical) equilibrium is laid down and, in the process, the baby develops an internal working model of the self as safe, special and valued.

Among the studies providing support for these ideas is one by Gunnar et al. (1992). They found heightened cortisol level in infants of 9 months of age half an hour after they had been separated from their main carer. If the substitute carer was interactive and responsive, cortisol levels reduced but they remained high in children with a carer who responded only to the baby's crying and did not interact otherwise, simply getting on with other tasks.

Attachment as a means of the child adapting to the environment

Remember how Bowlby was influenced by the ethologists and drew parallels between greylag geese imprinting on their mothers and human babies developing attachment bonds to theirs? In both cases, the behaviour is interpreted as having evolved to increase the young's chances of survival. This remains a useful way to view attachment (and other) behaviour. The human baby is dependent on others for a long period of time. The 'unfinished baby' (Gerhardt 2004) can grow and develop in a way that adapts to its surroundings. This is also consistent with socio-cultural models which emphasise that the form of development (in this case, the nature of the attachment bond) is determined by the interpersonal environment.

Reflection 2.1

- How can families be supported in developing secure attachments with their babies?
- How can we try to ensure that care and education of young children outside the home meet their attachment needs?

Key points

- Responsive 'mind-minded' parenting and caregiving by a limited number of people are important for the development of secure attachment which is associated with the best outcomes for children.
- A secure attachment to a practitioner (secondary attachment figure) does not threaten a child's attachment to the parents (primary attachment figures). The child benefits greatly from strong attachments to both.
- The Key Person role is about relationships. The quality of the relationship is determined by the extent to which the adult pays heed to the child's lead. Eye contact, facial expression, speed of movement and speech and tone of voice convey as much about the mutuality of a relationship as what is said.
- The more 'irritable' a young baby, the more the adult needs to soothe. Tiny babies cannot be 'spoiled'.
- Imitation is a powerful way of connecting to babies and children.
- Maintaining watchfulness over babies and young children is extremely important. They are attuned to the adults' reactions and will explore more if the adult is watching and is comfortable with what they are doing.
- Be wary of overwhelming parents with feelings that they should always respond and always interpret a baby's signals correctly. Embrace the concept of 'good enough' parenting for your interactions with parents.
- Use knowledge of attachment theory to try to help parents and children towards secure, fulfilling relationships and to support similar relationships in settings. Avoid making diagnoses or judgements and think instead in terms of how to promote security, positive interaction and close, responsive relationships for all children, in the setting and at home.

Further reading

Early Education supported by the Department for Education (2012) *Development Matters in the Early Years Foundation Stage (EYFS)*, London: Early Education.
Practitioners might find it helpful to reinforce the messages in this chapter by revisiting the PSE sections of *Development Matters*. The columns on 'what adults could do' and 'what adults could provide' are ways of translating attachment theory into practice.

Gerhardt, S. (2004) *Why Love Matters: How Affection Shapes a Baby's Brain*, Hove: Brunner-Routledge.
An easy-to-read book that carries a very powerful message about the importance of responsive early care.

3

Understanding insecure attachments and ways to help

'Understand that this behaviour started as self-protection'

Mary Ainsworth developed an understanding of insecure attachment patterns from her naturalistic studies but she is best known for her stroke of genius in devising the 'strange situation', an experimental set-up that provides a telling snapshot of attachment quality (Ainsworth 1978).

The 'strange situation'

Ainsworth brought mothers and their almost 1-year-old infants to the laboratory playroom, where the following sequence of events ensued, lasting about 20 minutes and observed through a one-way mirror.

- Mother and infant were alone in the playroom. Mother placed the child by the toys and herself went to a chair across the room (3 minutes).
- A stranger entered, sat (1 minute), talked to the mother (1 minute), then knelt on the floor to interact with the child (1 minute).
- Mother left, obeying an agreed signal.
- Stranger attempted to engage the child if s/he was not playing (3 minutes).
- Mother returned (Reunion 1) (3 minutes).
- Stranger left unobtrusively during Reunion 1.
- Mother left. The child was alone for up to 3 minutes (if not distressed).
- Stranger returned (3 minutes).
- Mother returned (Reunion 2).

Ainsworth devised the 'strange situation' primarily to produce experimental evidence that the infant–mother bond provides the infant with a secure base for play and exploration. She predicted that the 1-year-old children would play in the mother's presence as she would provide them with a safe base in the unfamiliar playroom. When she was not there, they would find the unfamiliar room a little threatening and play would subside, to be replaced with attachment behaviours such as crying and searching. The 'strange situation' did indeed demonstrate these factors. What proved to be most informative, however, was the range of responses to the two reunions with the mother. These responses Ainsworth was able to categorise into three main patterns, which correlated with what she knew of the same infants and mothers in their home situations and with her analyses of the interaction patterns observed naturalistically in both the Ugandan and the Baltimore studies. Later Mary Main, a colleague, added a fourth category, which will be included in the discussion (Main and Sullivan 1990). The 'strange situation' has been replicated extensively and proved to be a reliable indicator of attachment quality or type. Note the different behaviours associated with the attachment styles when we discuss them below. Interpreting behaviour through an 'attachment lens' can provide clues to whether a child's need for relatedness has been met in a healthy way.

Secure attachment

Securely attached infants take their cue from their mothers that it is fine to play. They are often distressed when their mother leaves but show obvious relief and pleasure in her return (the reunions). They seek proximity (closeness) to their mother when uncertain. When the stranger enters, they often approach their mother but they quickly pick up her cues that there is nothing to fear and are happy to resume play in the stranger's presence while their mother remains in the room.

Insecure attachment – avoidant

Avoidantly attached children appear to show no distress on their mother's departure though sometimes they look for her after she has gone. On reunion, they seem to show little response, ignoring their mother or possibly turning away from her. Their reunion behaviour seems to *avoid* proximity.

Avoidantly attached children seem to have developed an internal working model in which their carer is unreliable and they have to be self-sufficient (Figure 3.1). They seem to cope by 'dampening down' their needs and denying their vulnerability. They have not found relationships a source of fulfilment and are wary of them.

Interestingly, when Ainsworth first announced her findings, health professionals thought this was the most desirable form of attachment, construing these children as healthily independent. From her observational data in the home, however, Ainsworth knew that these children and parents had less attuned relationships than those who reacted in a secure manner. Ainsworth's feeling that all was not well with these children has been substantiated by physiological and longitudinal studies (for example, Maselko et al. 2011, discussed in Chapter 2). Avoidant attachment responses remind us that surface behaviour that seems 'good' (not

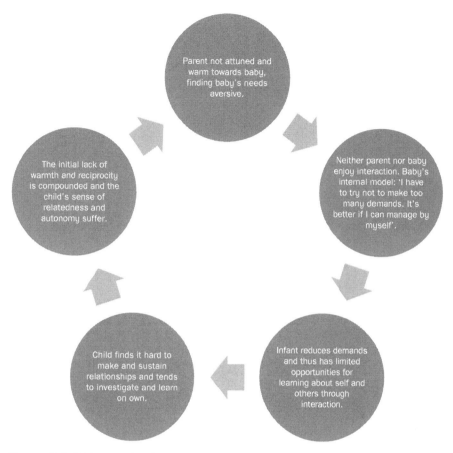

Figure 3.1 Vicious cycle of avoidant attachment

making demands on an adult) does not necessarily mean that all is well with a child. Practitioners should be alert for children who seem to lack emotion and shun connection with people.

Box 3.1: Theory into practice

Supporting children who appear very task-focused, unemotional and 'undemanding'

Consider:

• The Key Person making a special effort to institute regular periods of time with the child, building trust and shared pleasure. Focusing on a task or game the child likes may be a good starting point.

(Continued)

- Assessing and trying to build up the child's emotional understanding over time. Try brief periods of 'mind-minded' commentary. Gradually move to 'indirect' methods of developing emotional literacy using puppets or stories.
- Encouraging parents to share enjoyable activities with the child.
- Facilitating peer interaction by making opportunities for the child to play favourite games with another child.

Insecure attachment – ambivalent/resistant/anxious

Resistantly attached infants show mixed signals when reunited with their mothers. On the one hand, they seem to want to be close to her, on the other, they often show anger when she returns. When such children are picked up by their mothers, they might, for example, kick them until they are released. Their behaviour is *ambivalent*: they are both drawn to the mother but also *resist* proximity.

Children showing this pattern of insecure attachment develop an internal working model where they are unsure of their own worthiness and unsure about others' responses. In their anxiety to have relationships with others, they can sometimes make things backfire by being over-alert to threats, yet not registering positive signs. They can appear needy and constantly requiring reassurance.

Ainsworth's naturalistic observations again showed a lack of attunement at home between the infants and parents showing the resistant pattern in the 'strange situation'. In research carried out by Meins and her colleagues (Meins et al. 2012), resistant attachment at 15 months old was predicted when, at 8 months, the mothers made frequent non-attuned comments about their babies' presumed feelings, for example, 'You'd like this' and introducing another toy when the baby was fully engaged with the toy he already had or 'Come on, it's fun!' and continuing to operate a noisy toy near the baby's head when the baby was turning away.

Resistant attachment is associated with caregivers who are not consistently available to children and who are not sensitive to their needs. Towards one end of the ambivalent continuum, children tend to be hyper-vigilant, watching carers to determine their mood and the 'least bad' time to try to secure needed attention (Figure 3.2). These children may display a great deal of emotional behaviour and their anxiety and hostility may make it hard for them to get caught up in activities.

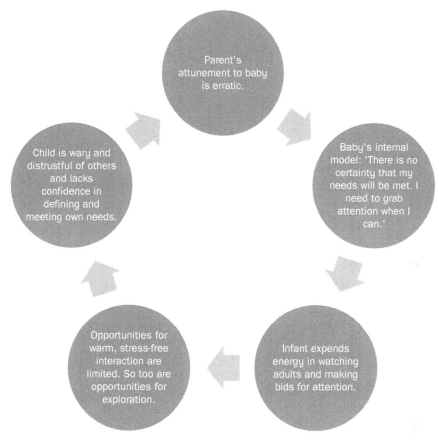

Figure 3.2 Vicious cycle of ambivalent/resistant attachment

Box 3.2: Theory into practice

Supporting children who appear watchful, hostile and poor at settling to activities

Consider:

- Emphasising the routines and predictability of the setting.
- Making sure all adults, but particularly the Key Person, are responsive in a calm and predictable manner.
- Observing the child's reactions and preferences and using a 'mind-minded' commentary to share tentative conclusions with the child.
- Tactfully sharing with the parents any strategies that appear to be working.

Case snippet 3.1: Lilly

Lilly, 2½ years old, has been attending the setting for several months but she and her mother still struggle at separation. Lilly clings to Mum and Mum exudes anxiety, and some impatience with Lilly. Lilly likes to stay close to Chris, her Key Person. When she is sitting next to Chris, she will have a go at some activities but she stops and follows Chris when he moves. When Chris takes a break, Lilly waits for him by the door where he will come back in, hanging her head and sucking her thumb. Other practitioners try to draw her into activities but with little success.

Chris is always warm towards Lilly, never showing any irritation with her constant presence beside him. On the few occasions when Lilly becomes fully immersed in an activity, he makes a mental note of what has captivated her (dressing up, hand painting, puppet play) but makes no comment. He simply ensures these activities are available to her and shares them with her frequently. When he leaves the room, he starts telling Lilly he is about to go, naming another member of staff who is available for her and saying he will find Lilly immediately on his return. At first, Lilly continues to wait by the door and Chris says, 'Lilly, remember I'll come and find you when I get back from my break, wherever you are.' Very gradually, Lilly becomes more involved in activities and will move around during Chris's absence. He is careful to make finding her his first priority on his return.

As Chris notes developments in Lilly's security, he gives Mum factual accounts of the strategies that seem to be helping: 'The last few days, Lilly has been happy to play when I'm on my break. For a while now, I've been saying to Lilly that Anna will look after her while I'm out and that I'll come and find her as soon as I'm back and now she seems to trust that I'll do this.' He hopes that by sharing and modelling strategies, Mum will be able to adopt them too.

Insecure attachment – disorganised or disoriented

This is the fourth category of attachment, added by Main (1996). It was used to describe insecure attachment that did not fit the other categories and which was bizarre or incorporated features of both avoidant and ambivalent responses. Some children seem to 'freeze' on reunion in the 'strange situation', others head towards their mother but then fall over, yet others lean their head against the wall (Main 1996). Whereas the other forms of insecure attachment have coherence to them, this is not true of disorganised attachment, which is indicative of the most severe damage in the attachment relationship.

Children who develop disorganised attachment are thought to have caregivers who are not only unpredictable but frightening or frightened (Main and Hesse 1990). Disorganised attachment has been shown in longitudinal studies to be a predictor of **externalising behaviour** problems (Lyons-Ruth 1996).

Practitioners will notice and be concerned about the behaviour of these children. They are likely to be angry and aggressive, controlling and unpredictable. Safeguarding concerns need to be at the forefront of everyone's minds.

Box 3.3: Theory into practice

Supporting children who shows extreme, 'acting out' behaviours
Aim to build children's sense of trust and security but in recognition that this is a particularly long and tough road for these children, consider:

- The possibility of a one-to-one Key Person working with only this child.
- Additional training or reading about disorganised attachment for as many members of staff as possible.
- A support network for the one-to-one Key Person, possibly daily short meetings with the manager and room staff to talk though progress, incidents and strategies. Both practical and emotional support will be crucial.

Note that all forms of attachment indicate a bond with the caregiver(s). Evolution has equipped babies to attach to their caregivers in the way that is likely to help them to survive longest. Avoidantly attached children try to minimise their demands on the caregiver whom they sense has limited capacity to help them – it is a survival strategy. Similarly, ambivalently attached children watch their caregivers very carefully as they fear that their needs will not be recognised if they do not remain alert to opportunities to 'present' them. Children are presumed to develop these styles because they are their best chance of having their needs met in the circumstances in which they find themselves. They are simply trying to protect themselves. When they later encounter different, more favourable, contingencies, as in attending a high quality childcare setting, they may struggle to accommodate. Patterns of behaviour are tied to patterns of physiological responses and can be hard to alter. Children's challenging behaviour is often a symptom of their confusion.

The descriptions of the insecure categories have indicated their associations with behaviour problems. Table 3.1 shows the links between attachment styles and behaviour.

Preventing or intervening early to help insecure attachment

Estimates of the prevalence of insecure attachment vary but claims are often made that 40 per cent of children may have insecure attachments (Moullin et al. 2014).

Certain categories of parents and children are at higher risk of insecure attachment. While being aware of these categories can help in the detection and prevention of, or support for, difficulties, it is crucial not to jump to conclusions without considering each family in the round, including strengths and buffers as well as risk factors.

Table 3.1 Summary of attachment styles and behaviours

	Behaviour in the 'strange situation'		'Internal working model'	Associated feelings and behaviours in the longer term
	In mother's absence	Reunions		
Secure attachment	I cry and am distressed.	I'm pleased to see Mummy. I smile at her and we hug and then I'm fine to play again.	'I can rely on Mummy to look after me.	I like making friends, I love exploring and playing and I'm happy to be me.
Insecure avoidant attachment	You won't notice anything wrong with me. I might look for Mummy.	I don't show much reaction. Possibly I'll turn away from Mummy.	Mummy doesn't notice or gets irritated if I need help.	It's safest if I manage by myself as much as possible myself. Mummy has so much else to cope with. I just need to hold it together. Sometimes I get angry with other people.
Insecure ambivalent/ resistant attachment	I'm very upset when Mummy leaves.	I go to Mummy but I'm a bit angry. I'm certainly going to stay right by her.	I need to be vigilant so that I can work out the least bad times to get my needs met.	I need to be constantly on my guard to work out when it might be safe to try to get my needs met. It's exhausting and takes up most of my energy. I'm often anxious and sometimes angry inside.
Insecure disorganised attachment	It's not easy to predict what I'll do.	I might freeze or rock.	I never quite know how Mummy will react. Sometimes I'm scared of her.	I don't understand myself or other people very well. I try to control things because so much in my life is uncontrollable. I'm confused, angry and aggressive.

Factors associated with an increased risk of insecure attachment include: maternal depression (Martins and Gaffen 2000); other mental health problems in the family including alcohol or drug dependency; poverty; young age of mother; parents' own experience of insecure attachment; and the child experiencing multiple caregivers and poor quality childcare (van IJzendoorn et al.1999; Thompson 2013). Of course, these factors may overlap, for example, a young mother may be poor and suffer from depression and may also use a variety of caregivers of variable quality.

Socio-economic or mental health category is not destiny. For children, the key factor seems to be whether they receive responsive care. The support parents in difficult circumstances receive is crucial. Remember also that some babies (those with 'difficult temperaments') seem to be more susceptible to adverse outcomes if care is suboptimal so the parents of 'irritable' babies may need particular support. None of the 'risk factors' doom a child to insecure attachment. There are, for example, depressed parents who 'defy the statistics' and are responsive and promote active problem-solving in their children (Nolen-Hoeksema et al. 1995).

The Introduction to Part 1 made reference to parents' own attachment status as judged by the Adult Attachment Interview (AAI) (Main 1996). The ways that adults are categorised in the AAI have been mapped on to the 'strange situation' classifications at infancy (Main 1996). Main reports that the adult category matches to the infant (secure versus insecure but not which particular form of insecure) about 75 per cent of the time.

The AAI encourages interviewees to describe their own attachment experiences and provide examples to illustrate these descriptions. The interview takes about an hour and categorisation is based on the coherence of the dialogue around their personal experiences. Importantly, individuals may have had quite challenging early attachment experiences but nevertheless might fall in the healthiest 'secure autonomous' category if they have integrated their experience and believe in and value positive relationships. It is their mental representations that are significant and some people seem to have altered their representations in the light of subsequent experience. This is a positive finding and points to the preventative and remedial work that can help families. People whose AAI scores suggest they are vulnerable to promoting insecure attachment in their children could be helped before they become parents, an enticing prospect for those working with parents ante-natally. Working with existing parents to help them make sense of their own experience and to promote their children's security is, rightly, a current focus in many children's centres and among professionals supporting children and families. Interventions that increase parents' sensitivity to their children have proved successful (Bakermans-Kranburg et al. 2003).

Childcare settings and insecure attachment

Low quality childcare threatens children's secure attachment and their well-being. Babies and children may be outwardly calm in relatively unresponsive settings but this may mask underlying problems, for example, Dettling et al. (1999) found elevated cortisol levels (a sign of stress) in 3- and 4-year-olds in nursery though their behaviour caused no concern. Rapid turnover of staff, long work shifts and tokenistic implementation of the Key Person requirement are among the correlations of low quality childcare. Managers should guard against these factors, including ensuring that work patterns are not so extreme that practitioners tend to become listless and relatively unresponsive towards the end of long shifts. Chapter 2 looked in depth at ways in which settings can promote secure attachment.

Depression (and other risk factors) may affect not just parents but also practitioners. Managers should be alert to any such factors and discuss and acknowledge the possible effort that affected practitioners may need to exert, and the support they may require, to deliver suitably responsive care.

Using an 'attachment lens': some provisos

Attachment categories are useful for highlighting different possible developmental pathways but remember that they may imply more clear-cut categories than are the reality for many children. Each category will cover a continuum of reactions and not all children in the insecure categories will have problems. Children may have a different style of attachment to each parent. Also, of course, events such as the birth of a sibling, separation of parents or a family bereavement are likely to have at least a temporary impact on even a very securely attached child, as do states such as tiredness and illness. Attachment history but also current experiences shape the future trajectory of someone's relationships, well-being and behaviour (Thompson 2013).

The 'strange situation' has been useful for giving an indicator of attachment style. The 'strange situation' is designed for mothers and their 1-year-old babies. Children's response to being left in a setting is not the same as a 'strange situation' response. Be aware that children's age, familiarity with leaving the parent and a host of other factors will impact on a child's reaction.

Staff in settings should be informed and vigilant about the risk groups and possible indicators of insecure attachment yet it is important to avoid hasty judgements and stereotyping of families. Safeguarding concerns must be acted on speedily and with regard to the statutory guidance (DfE 2013, 2014b). In the absence of such concerns, a purely supportive approach is advocated. Practitioners should inform themselves of local sources of support for parents and signpost them accordingly. Non-stigmatising activities that encourage attunement between parent and child (such as 'baby massage' or 'rhyme time') can be beneficial.

Key points

- Ainsworth's 'strange situation' led to the identification of patterns of insecure attachment, each with implications for the internal working model a child forms which then influences subsequent relationships and behaviour:

- Avoidant attachment where children behave 'well' but are wary of relationships, self-sufficient and at risk of not developing sensitivity to others which could have repercussions for their behaviour as they develop.
- Resistant, ambivalent or anxious attachment where children have had their needs met only intermittently. They are very vigilant and uncertain in relationships and not sure of their own worth. They can be regarded as 'clingy', 'attention-seeking' and 'needy'.
- Disorganised attachment which does not follow a coherent pattern and is associated with the most worrying and challenging behaviour. These children may have been frightened by their caregivers and are very confused and needy. Safeguarding must be borne in mind. Individual packages of care are likely to be necessary.

- Risk factors for the development of insecure attachment are known but each child and family needs to be considered as an individual system, with strengths and buffers as well as risk factors.
- Parents can be helped to develop responsiveness to, and understanding of, their children's needs and this can impact positively on outcomes.
- Attachment history is important but relationships can improve in quality with help, new relationships can provide healthier models and positive experiences can impact on a child's internal working model. The fact that some adults scoring in the most favourable category of the Adult Attachment Interview did so despite poor early attachment experiences shows that positive change is possible. This is the goal for those trying to help children and families.

Further reading

Bomber, L.M. (2007) *Inside I'm Hurting: Practical Strategies for Supporting Children with Attachment Difficulties in Schools*, London: Worth Publishing.

Bomber, L.M. (2011) *What about Me? Inclusive Strategies to Support Pupils with Attachment Difficulties Make It through the School Day*, London: Worth Publishing.

Geddes, H. (2006) *Attachment in the Classroom: The Links between Children's Early Experience, Emotional Well-Being and Performance in Schools*, London: Worth Publishing.

Heather Geddes and Louise Bomber are two writers who address the impact of insecure attachment on behaviour in schools and strategies to help. Their work is focused on school-aged children but might nevertheless be of interest for they give clear depictions of the ongoing challenges faced by children with insecure attachment. They explain the difficulties empathetically and advocate positive practical approaches.

Part 2
Autonomy

'Being me'

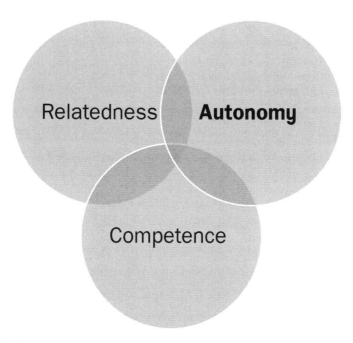

Figure P2.1 The three psychological needs: focus on autonomy
Source: Based on Deci and Ryan (2000).

Introduction to Part 2

Autonomy is to do with being true to oneself. In self-determination theory (Deci and Ryan 2000, 2002) the need for autonomy is considered to be lifelong. It is also universal though it may be expressed slightly differently in different cultures with, broadly speaking, more individualistic expression in Western societies and more alignment with community activities in collectivist cultures. Skinner and Edge (2002) argue that autonomy is just as important as relatedness and competence in determining how effectively people cope with adversity but has not received the same recognition. According to Koestner and Losier's interpretation of self-determination theory: 'the need for autonomy is the most central nutrient to the person's growth' (2002: 106).

Before turning to how babies and young children develop a sense of autonomy, it can be useful to take a broader look at autonomy, from readers' perspectives as adults. What does the healthy expression of autonomy look like? Which factors promote the healthy expression and which factors lead to a less healthy expression of this need? Consider the bullet points below which summarise the view of autonomy as portrayed in Deci and Ryan's (2000) self-determination theory. Developing a clear view of healthy adult autonomy can provide a useful context for valuing the development of autonomy in young children. By taking the longer view, we can see the importance of promoting autonomy in young children and recognise some behaviours as a necessary part of its development.

Autonomous individuals

- Know their own minds and feel able to be their genuine selves.
- Make their own choices.
- Act in a manner consonant with their beliefs and values.
- Are open to their emotions but not at their mercy.
- Cherish their relationships and feel any compromises they make for the sake of relationships are outweighed by their value.
- Can negotiate flexibly, maintaining a focus on priorities and compromising on other matters.
- Have a sense of vitality and growth.

What autonomy is not

- Being totally independent and self-centred.
- Feeling a need to control everything and everyone.
- Always having to be right and get things right.

Autonomy-supporting environments

- Are respectful of everyone.
- Acknowledge feelings (and help people to recognise their own feelings).
- Allow choice.
- Require tasks for a good reason and make the reason clear.
- Allow people a say (and act upon that say).
- Recognise the contributions people make.
- Model successful conflict resolution and negotiation.
- Allow people to try things and accept that mistakes will happen and can be learning experiences.
- Allow risk taking.
- Are set up so that people can take some initiative.
- Give appropriate opportunities for responsibility.
- Provide 'structured freedom'.

Environments that undermine autonomy: harsh

- Are hierarchical and dismissive of those low in the hierarchy.
- Ignore feelings.
- Control by domineering – threats, surveillance, evaluation, deadlines.
- Make seemingly arbitrary demands ('Because I say so!')
- Discourage expression of views and become more intransigent in demands if negative views are expressed.
- Ignore or belittle contributions.
- Model imposition of one's will.
- Insist on things being done a certain way and punish when things go wrong.
- May at times force people to take risks that scare them.
- Either allow no initiative in tasks or require an unreasonable amount of initiative (undermining competence).
- Give inappropriate levels of responsibility.
- Compel people to do as directed

Environments that undermine autonomy: stifling

• Acknowledge people but with condescension or 'smothering'.
• Deny negative feelings. ('Of course you don't hate her, you're friends!')
• Make choices for other people.
• Give reasons for tasks that are to do with (extrinsic) rewards on completion.
• Do not seek opinions or do not take opinions seriously.
• Praise and talk positively all the time and indiscriminately.
• Model a superficial 'we all have only positive emotions' way of dealing with situations.
• Intervene to ensure things are done the 'best' way and success is assured.
• Protect from risks.
• Provide support to the extent that initiative is not required.
• Do not offer responsibility.
• Limit freedom, even though there may be a range of stimulating activities.

Reflection P2.1: Feelings of autonomy

Reflect on the definition of autonomy given above. Consider to what degree you feel autonomous. This may vary in different contexts and your feelings of autonomy are likely to have varied at different times in your life. To what extent have you experienced autonomy-supporting or autonomy-undermining environments? Reflect with regard to the following:

• the home you grew up in;
• your education;
• your current living arrangements;
• your workplace.

Autonomy in the early years

Supporting the development of autonomy is not at all to do with giving children free rein to do what they want. Rather, it is about helping them to recognise their unique selves and supporting them in finding ways of participating in their culture while also meeting their own psychological needs. Autonomous individuals feel they can be themselves while also being part of groups, be they families, settings or schools. They feel that they make their own choices about how to behave as opposed to being constrained to behave in certain ways. Skinner and Edge (2002: 298) define autonomy as 'the need to express one's authentic self and to experience that self as the source of action'. They see autonomy as the opposite of coercion. Coercion comes in myriad forms. It is easily recognised in (the fear of) harsh punishment but it can also be experienced in other ways, including fear of loss of love and pressure of others' expectations. Over-protection and intrusive helpfulness (so-called 'helicopter parenting') can be coercive as they constrain people's options.

The degree of autonomy experienced by children impacts upon how they internalise the expectations and demands that are increasingly placed on them as they grow up. Deci and Ryan argue that **socialisation** and **internalisation** are natural processes. Provided their psychological needs are met, children's sense of relatedness will lead them to internalise the 'demands' of their culture (the things that they have to do that are not intrinsically appealing).

Autonomy develops over time as children learn about themselves and about the society in which they are growing up. Some 'aggressive' and 'defiant' behaviour (terms used in the psychological literature and hence used here) is perhaps usefully construed as part of the natural development of autonomy. Other, more persistent and extreme behaviour could be interpreted by the Deci and Ryan (2000) model as a reaction against an environment that undermines the development of autonomy. A child who is very aggressive towards adults and children may be reacting to a harsh, coercive and punitive environment.

One of the major insights offered by the model is that some children whose behaviour is not seen as causing concern may be storing up problems for the future because their sense of autonomy is not being nurtured. People at different ends of the autonomy continuum might behave equally 'well' but the motivations behind their behaviour might have vastly different consequences for their well-being and their behaviour in the future. Think of the case where children say 'sorry' to another child after a dispute because the other child's upset reaction makes them realise that they acted unfairly and the child's reaction is legitimate. This is completely different from a case where a child says 'sorry' out of fear or social expectation yet is really the wronged partner but cannot express this or has no expectation of being listened to. The former is autonomous behaviour with children choosing freely to adopt the social custom of apology; the latter behaviour is 'controlled', motivated by others' expectations but not 'true' to the child's inner self.

There are various different strands of research with a bearing on how children develop autonomy. They offer different perspectives though there is some overlap and certainly some commonality in the lessons offered for effective autonomy-supporting practice. The structure of Part 2 on autonomy is as follows:

- Chapter 4 – 'Boundary setting: "I need to explore and find out about the world and myself within managed boundaries"'. This chapter emphasises the importance of parents setting boundaries for children. It explores the literature on parenting styles to help practitioners understand how particular patterns of child behaviour result from particular styles. Practitioners are in a strong position to support parents with setting boundaries. The chapter also suggests ways in which autonomy can be supported within the setting.

- Chapter 5 – 'Emotions: "I need to understand my own feelings and how to use them constructively"'. This chapter explains why emotions have an important role in the development of autonomy. It emphasises that negative emotions should not be denied or ignored. It describes and advocates 'emotion coaching' (Gottman with Declaire 1997) as a constructive approach to fostering emotional awareness and hence autonomy.
- Chapter 6 – 'Unique but belonging: "I want to be me but I still need to be loved"'. This chapter investigates the toddler's journey towards autonomy, giving guidance on typical development to inform interpretation of behaviour. It also presents the research evidence on what adults can do to support the journey toward autonomy, giving practical examples.

Autonomy and the EYFS

While the term 'autonomy' does not appear in the EYFS, ideas related to the concept do feature, as shown in Box P2.1.

Box P2.1: Autonomy and the EYFS

- One of the four overarching principles is that 'every child is a unique child, who is constantly learning and can be resilient, capable, confident and self-assured'. Promoting autonomy is to do with helping children appreciate and express their unique qualities while also belonging to communities.
- The designation of PSE as a prime area of learning and development emphasises its importance. PSE includes the following aspects, all of which link to developing autonomy:
  - 'Helping children to develop a positive sense of themselves.'
  - Children 'say why they like some activities more than others.'
  - They 'choose the resources they need for their chosen activities.'
  - 'They say when they do or don't need help.'
- Learning related to autonomy is likely to be threaded throughout the curriculum. The EYFS (DfE 2014b) includes relevant material in the guidance on 'Understanding the world: people and communities': children 'know that other children don't always enjoy the same things, and are sensitive to this' (DfE 2014b).

4

Boundary setting

'I need to explore and find out about the world and myself within managed boundaries'

Young children require structure if they are to develop autonomy. Reasonable behavioural boundaries or limits provide structure and support development. The purpose of boundaries should be to allow safe, harmonious living for all, without cramping or restraining anyone unduly. Young babies, as we have seen, benefit from attentive, responsive care but carers need to adapt their support to the growing capacities of a child. If a mother who immediately fed a hungry baby and who quickly retrieved her young baby's dropped toy is reacting the same way two years later, the outcome would most likely be an exhausted mother and a tyrannical child. The importance of boundaries is emphasised by recent work which draws on research to identify the strongest predictors of positive outcomes for children (Roberts and Donkin 2014). Setting and reinforcing boundaries features among the 21 strongest predictors.

Gralinski and Kopp (1993) carried out a study investigating the 'everyday rules for behaviour' adopted by 71 mothers as their infants grew. The results suggested that mothers tend to support their children's **socialisation** over time by increasing the number and scope of rules as children develop (Table 4.1). Repetition of rules, and initial adult intervention to enforce the rules were a normal part of the process before, over time, children generally followed the rules most of the time without prompting. This study, while not producing surprising results,

Table 4.1 Everyday rules for behaviour

Age of child	Rules cover
Under 1 year	Safety
13 months	As above plus not hurting others, not damaging things, waiting for attention or food
18 months	As above plus manners and mealtime routines

Source: Based on Gralinski and Kopp (1993).

captures the way most mothers were, in effect, treating children like young apprentices to a culture and helping them gradually develop the behaviours to fit in. Reasonable boundaries and rules provide the 'structured freedom' that promotes autonomy. Accepting that children need support and will only gradually become consistent in adhering to rules is another autonomy-supporting factor.

For children, appropriate, managed boundaries fulfil several important purposes. They supply them with a safe and predictable framework for playing and living. At the same time they provide areas for children to test out their influence and power, a natural part of being curious and learning about oneself and relationships. Boundaries also give children the message that certain types of behaviour are expected here – it prepares them for restrictions they will come across in different places and gives them a prototype against which to compare and contrast other systems they encounter in the future. Managed boundaries show children that someone is noticing them and, though there will be occasions when they wish this was not so, the underlying message they absorb is that they are worth noticing, they *matter*.

Parenting/child-rearing styles

'Parenting styles' capture patterns of parent behaviour. The patterns are made up of a number of different parental behaviours and the motivations that seem to underlie them. The styles are composite categories, amalgams of different elements. They stereotype the different styles to some extent but are useful to set the scene and give a broad analysis of how different child-rearing approaches promote or hinder autonomy and positive behaviour in the long term. In this chapter, the emphasis is placed on boundary setting for children, an issue of crucial importance in promoting positive behaviour but something that can be problematical for parents and often plays a part in children's behavioural difficulties. Many loving parents fail to put in appropriate boundaries, possibly construing themselves as kind and tolerant. Boundaries, appropriately set and managed, play a vital role in helping children feel safe and promoting autonomy. Children thrive when life is predictable and there is the safety of adults being in overall control. The discussion on attachment theory stressed that babies who are soothed and comforted go on to regulate their own emotions. Similarly, children brought up with reasonable boundaries learn to impose boundaries on their own behaviour. They are less likely to mismanage the freedoms of adolescence than their peers brought up with unduly restrictive boundaries or virtually no boundaries.

Research on parenting styles is relevant for practitioners. If they understand the types of behaviour associated with each style, this can provide a basis for interpreting children's behaviour and for working with families to promote an alternative style, when appropriate. Where families have established few boundaries, one of the most important contributions practitioners can make is to help parents understand the value of boundary setting and to support them in the difficult task of putting in limits when a child has become accustomed to operating without them. A further reason for practitioners to know about parenting styles is that the style associated with best outcomes for children is also relevant for best practice in education and childcare settings.

Landmark work on families and boundaries was carried out by Diana Baumrind in 1966 but the basic outline of her findings and insights remains current, with subsequent research refining rather than radically revising her ideas. Baumrind (1966) reviewed 12 studies into parent behaviour and its effects on children. She selected studies where the children had been observed directly and on a number of occasions. Some had been observed at home or in school, others in laboratory settings. The parents had been interviewed about their attitudes and behaviour. Some studies also involved direct observation of the parents' interaction styles. From analysing the studies, Baumrind concluded that parenting styles could be divided into three broad types (though she recognised that a given parent would probably use different styles at different times): authoritarian; permissive; and authoritative.

Authoritarian parenting

Authoritarian parents are highly controlling of their children, setting firm boundaries to suit their own desires and/or beliefs and not seeing any need to take the children's views into account. Boundaries are strictly enforced, sometimes by threat of, or actual, physical punishment. This is the 'spare the rod and spoil the child' view of parenting where children are believed to have to shape up to high expectations for their own good. Authoritarian parents prize obedience and conformity. They (or the higher sources that guide them, for example, religious ideas) know what is right and children are discouraged from debating, avoiding or transgressing the rules. The rules are the rules and need no explanation. The authoritarian style is harshly undermining of autonomy.

Children in authoritarian households are likely to be expected to help substantially with jobs around the house. Often there is no choice over the types of jobs carried out or when they are done.

Authoritarian parenting is associated with children who look to adults to organise their lives. They lack opportunities to develop autonomy. 'Good' behaviour is enforced and children brought up by authoritarian parents are often compliant. Particularly when harsh physical or psychological punishment has been involved, children tend to respond in one of two ways. Their response might be hostile withdrawal (retreating into themselves, not engaging with others or with activities, being nervous, possibly flinching if someone makes a sudden gesture in their direction). On the other hand, children treated in this way may 'act out' when away from their parents, hitting and trying to control other children, using some of the tactics they have themselves experienced. There is evidence that coercive, authoritarian parenting of babies is associated with challenging behaviour by the child later on (for example, Tremblay et al. 2004).

Permissive parenting

Baumrind's characterisation of permissive parenting, while based on research, is influenced by the sociocultural environment in which she was working – 1960s America, the 'Swinging Sixties', a time of experimentation with relationships and of rapid change in society.

Permissive parents are portrayed as loving and giving, to a fault. They are accepting of their children and act as though they want to be their friend rather than their parent. Their underlying view (of which they may not be conscious) is of themselves as someone to help their children by granting their wishes to a large degree. They do not see their key roles as being to provide a role model for their children or to guide and mould their behaviour. They make few demands on their children, wanting to provide them with space and opportunity to be themselves and to grow into their own aspirations. These parents may intend to afford children autonomy but the evidence of the effect of this style is otherwise. Permissive parents avoid exerting control but will try to reason with children. If that fails, they may use what Baumrind terms 'manipulation', for example, diversionary tactics. Permissive parents tend not to set explicit boundaries for children. Children hold a great deal of control in households where the dominant style is permissive. What they lack is a developmentally appropriate level of structure to provide the levels of predictability and security that might enable them to exercise this control in a constructive and autonomous fashion.

Permissive parents typically expect their children to do few chores in the household as they grow up.

Permissive parenting is associated with children who find it hard to understand that rules in settings and schools apply to them as well as everyone else. These children may defy rules, ignore what adults say and argue with those who try to get them to conform to behavioural expectations. They can be lacking in initiative and tend to expect adults to solve their problems for them. Practitioners and teachers (and, sometimes, parents) may view such children as 'difficult' and unruly. The children lack the confidence, the security and the positive, goal-focused approach that might have been fostered in them. They tend to expend a great deal of energy trying to sort out the sometimes overpowering extent of their control. They can be confused by the conflicting expectations placed on them at home and elsewhere.

Regarding 'permissive' approaches, it is important for both parents and practitioners to be aware that when an adult is present but does not intervene to set appropriate boundaries on behaviour, children seem to assume that what they are doing is being condoned – the chances of them repeating behaviour with negative consequences for others are higher than if no adult had been present (Siegel and Kohn 1959; Singer and de Haan 2007: 44). This emphasises the importance of adults maintaining appropriate boundaries. Not to do so is a missed opportunity for promoting positive behaviour but, more than this, it may worsen behaviour.

Case snippet 4.1: Piotr

Piotr is a lively, watchful boy with a winning smile. His Dad brings him to nursery each day and is pleasant and friendly with the staff. Piotr's behaviour often seems to embarrass Dad. Piotr sometimes pulls Dad away when he is talking to the Key Person. Dad will say, 'Just a minute, Piotr', but Piotr shouts, 'No! Now!' and Dad gets pulled away, smiling apologetically. Once Piotr hit Dad when he arrived to collect him, saying, 'You put cheese in my sandwich! Naughty Daddy!' There have been other such instances. At the setting, Piotr is gradually learning to follow the routines such as joining other children on the carpet and sitting at the table for a snack. He will sometimes join in tidying up but this has to be prompted. His relations with other children are uneasy. He seems to want to play with them and sometimes manages this successfully for a time but often he bosses them about and seems to struggle to accept other people's ideas. The Key Person is thinking about asking to meet Dad without Piotr present to ask about Piotr's behaviour at home and to explore the issue of boundaries.

Authoritative parenting

Authoritative parents see their role as guiding children and, over time, they hope to help their children develop into young people who manage their own behaviour, taking into account its effects on others. These parents set boundaries but not in an arbitrary fashion. They are happy to articulate the reasons for the boundaries and, as children grow up, they will be open to discussion and flexibility on some boundaries. Crucial boundaries, for example, to do with safety, might be varied with the age of the child but be otherwise non-negotiable.

Authoritative parents typically expect children to take on some responsibility for jobs in the home but may offer a degree of choice concerning the jobs and some flexibility in when they are carried out.

Children of authoritative parents are those that are best equipped to develop autonomy and flourish in the settings and schools of Western democracies. This parenting style is associated with responsible children, who conform the majority of the time but may speak up if they feel something is unfair. They tend to have confidence in the value of their ideas and opinions but listen to, and value, other opinions too. These children usually co-operate with others. They play an active role in solving any problems they face but they will seek adult support appropriately.

There is some evidence to suggest that authoritative parenting enables babies with 'difficult temperaments' to overcome the association between this temperament and behaviour difficulties in pre-school (Paulssen-Hoogeboom et al. 2008). Differences in children's temperaments exist and babies and young children considered to have a 'difficult temperament' are those who tend to display powerful negative emotions such as sadness, frustration and anger. Authoritative parenting helps such children. This links with evidence that responsive caregiving mitigates against 'difficult temperament' resulting in externalising behaviour difficulties (Kochanska and Sanghag 2013).

Baumrind's categories of parental attitudes and behaviour and their effects on children are useful for informing practice and reflection. Two notes of caution need to be sounded. The first is the likely cultural specificity of the ideas. Our settings and schools prize certain characteristics and, in our culture, a particular parenting style (authoritative) promotes children's likelihood of developing the required characteristics. In other cultures, the findings are more ambivalent. The second note of caution is somewhat related to the first but also raises the issue of 'values' versus 'research evidence'. Some people are shocked to find that Baumrind is not completely against physical punishment. Whilst abhorring harsh punishment, she believes there is evidence that mild physical punishment may have some benefits. Here her views are at odds with prevailing norms in the world of British education. We perhaps need to acknowledge that there is an important place for 'values-led' approaches as well as for evidence-based ones. Hopefully the two approaches work in tandem but this is not always the case. (A strong argument can, however, be made that 'benefits' achieved by mild physical punishment can be better achieved in alternative ways.)

In her discussion of parenting styles and their effects, Baumrind makes implicit reference to a hostility/warmth continuum. Hostile control by a parent is the authoritarian style. Firm control by a warm parent is the authoritative style. The context of particular actions/attitudes – the relationships within which they occur – are all-important. This is why there is an overlap between relatedness and autonomy (see Figure P2.1). Just as both parent and baby thrive and benefit from secure attachment in the baby stage, so too does authoritative parenting protect both from the long-term damage that can occur if boundaries/behavioural limits are not negotiated in a way that meets both sets of needs. Within the authoritative relationship, children have a strong sense of security and belonging in the home and a strong drive to please their parents. Authoritative parents are attuned to a child's feelings and developing competencies, while also recognising their own needs and those of all in the household. Both parent and child derive pleasure from their relationship. These factors hold fundamentally true even though children – as a natural part of their curiosity and learning – will test any boundaries they face.

In later reviews of parenting styles, researchers have identified an overprotection/coercive control continuum in addition to the hostility/warmth one (Parker 1983; Chorpita and Barlow 1998). These continua relate well to the ideas in this book regarding the environments that promote satisfaction of the need for autonomy. Both ends of the overprotection/control continuum are associated with limiting autonomy. Over-protective parents limit children's opportunities to learn about the consequences of their behaviour and about how to manage the risks they take. This may be a parental practice that is increasing among recent generations of parents. Certainly, providers of early years education and care and local authorities responsible for playgrounds have been influenced by health and safety concerns and awareness of legal repercussions should anything go wrong. Reasonable precautions must be taken but, equally, children need developmentally appropriate opportunities to stretch themselves and exercise their capabilities to the limit.

Case snippet 4.2: Millie

Millie always arrives at pre-school in a pretty dress and with her hair beautifully groomed and tied with ribbons to match her dress. She plays very happily in the role play area and with the small world toys. She sometimes chooses a bike and she enjoys climbing on the outside apparatus. She gets on well with other children and practitioners like her and have no concerns about her. Ruth, her Key Person, notices that Millie steadfastly avoids any messy activities though sometimes she notices her looking at the water tray, the painting corner and the mud kitchen as though she might like to take part. Any time Millie is invited to take part in a messy activity, she shakes her head and moves away. Ruth wonders if Millie is worried about her dress. She mentions to Mum that children are supposed to come in old clothes so that getting messy is not a problem. Millie's Mum says it's fine, Millie doesn't like messy play and prefers to stay clean and look nice. Not convinced, Ruth offers Millie and some of her friends the opportunity to change into some old clothes belonging to the nursery. She tells them they can get as messy as they like and there will be time to wash them thoroughly and change into their clothes before the parents come. Millie is a little hesitant and at first goes to play with the small world toys. Later, however, she chooses to paint. Ruth is pleased and repeats the experiment once a week. Millie gradually becomes more comfortable with messy play. Ruth realises she needs to talk to Mum and gently explain how Millie has been influenced by Mum's preference (neat and tidy, no mess) to the extent of limiting her exploration, play and learning. Ruth is tempted not to raise this tricky topic but realises she must try since Mum is probably not deliberately stifling Millie's autonomy. If Mum can be convinced that it is in Millie's long-term interests to let her try activities that are not Mum's own preferred ones, then Millie will benefit.

Child-rearing styles that are lacking in warmth (relatively non-responsive to children's bids for attention) and at the same time over-protective are thought to render children susceptible to anxiety disorders (Parker 1983). Parker characterises this situation as one of 'affectionless control'. This is a situation that could occur in childcare settings of low quality, to the great detriment of the children concerned.

The term 'reasonable' has been repeatedly used in this chapter with reference to rules and boundaries. Arbitrary rules militate against autonomy. Of course, rules may seem reasonable to their originator and appear arbitrary to those expected to follow them! Explaining rules and boundaries to children supports effective internalisation and autonomy – children can, for example, choose to be kind to other children, recognising how being unkind to them would make them feel. This is much more autonomous than acting in 'a kind way' to avoid negative consequences of not doing so. Involving children in deciding the rules in a setting can be an important part of supporting autonomy.

Box 4.1: Theory into practice

Supporting autonomy through boundaries, rules and routines in early years settings

The boundaries, rules and routines should be:

- *Clear*. How do children know about them? Do some children benefit from visual or 'social story' ways of sharing the rules (Gray 2001; Box 8.1)? How are young children helped to remember the rules? Are they rehearsed? Is there some form of age-appropriate display? Is the number of rules tailored to children's memory capacity?
- *Useful and explicable (i.e. not arbitrary)*. Can you explain the rule in a way the children can understand the need for it?
- *Consistently applied*. What happens when rules are infringed? The Goldilocks principle is apposite – not too little reaction, not too much, just the right response to be effective in increasing the likelihood a child will conform to the rule in the future.
- *Drawn up with child involvement*. Is there age-appropriate discussion about rules and appropriate incorporation of children's ideas? Is care taken to try to ascertain the views and preferences of non-verbal children?

Key points

- Authoritative parenting (and childrearing practice) promote the development of autonomy.
- 'Structured freedom' involves providing reasonable behavioural boundaries with the reasons explained to the child, as well as opportunities for developmentally appropriate choice and risk-taking.
- Some parents may benefit from advice and support regarding boundary-setting. Acknowledge that putting in boundaries late is hard work and support parents with this task, stressing the long-term benefits for all the family.
- Harsh, coercive control impedes the development of autonomy but so too does over-protection.

- Developmentally appropriate choices and responsibility can promote autonomy.
- Adults need to step in when they observe children behaving inappropriately. While they should allow time for children to settle their own disputes, 'turning a blind eye' to behaviour that overrides another child's rights is interpreted as condoning the behaviour and thus may lead to more such behaviour in the future.
- 'Affectionless overprotection' sows the seeds for future behavioural problems derived from anxiety. A robotic, soulless implementation of legislative requirements could result in this style of provision.

Further reading

Early Education supported by the Department for Education (2012) *Development Matters in the Early Years Foundation Stage (EYFS)*, London: Early Education.
Practitioners might find it helpful to look at the section in *Development Matters* on PSE: Managing Feelings and Behaviour and to find the links with setting boundaries.

Roberts, R. (2006) *Self-Esteem and Early Learning: Key People from Birth to School*, 3rd edn, London: Paul Chapman.
Chapter 6 is on the topic of adults setting limits.

5

Emotions
'I need to understand my own feelings and how to use them constructively'

An important part of autonomy involves recognising emotions and being able to use them as a helpful guide to action, thus avoiding the situation where negative emotions build up and 'hijack' a person, whether this comes out as an explosion of anger or a complete withdrawal from a relationship in hurt and frustration. Emotions and behaviour have strong links. Supporting autonomy in children includes helping them to understand their emotions.

Emotions: why have they evolved?

From an evolutionary viewpoint, the wide range of emotions that humans experience must have given our ancestors a survival advantage. The positive emotions of happiness, joy and love build attachment and strengthen relationships – in evolutionary terms, this was necessary to maintain bonds over the time taken to raise children. Positive emotions also maximise our learning capacities, key for adapting and surviving. The negative emotions such as fear, anger, jealousy and anxiety act to register threat. In our evolutionary history it will have been advantageous to get away from a fear-inducing predator, to fight off anyone or anything threatening our young, to act against a rival for our mate and to be cautious and protect ourselves, our family and belongings when faced with uncertainty of any sort. Shame and guilt will have promoted behaviour to cement the social group, limit deviant behaviour and keep everyone safe.

The standard evolutionary argument for the enormous capacity of the human brain is that it was advantageous (and therefore selected) because it enhanced survival by making possible technological advances, but an alternative view (Humphrey 1976) is that the social demands of human life were the driver for the complexity and capability of the human brain. Living and working in social groups brings huge benefits but also requires constant balancing of one's own and others' needs in ever shifting and never completely predictable situations (a balancing act that Deci and Ryan would say requires self-determined autonomous behaviour). Humphrey's argument stresses the 'social function of intellect' (Humphrey 1976). Emotions, if read correctly, can be invaluable tools that enable us to navigate our socially complex worlds.

Case snippet 5.1: Ivan

Ivan, 4 years old, has a funny feeling in his tummy and keeps feeling hot and bothered. Mum asks him what is wrong and he says he doesn't know. He says his tummy feels funny and Mum says, 'You're starting school tomorrow. You'll love it but of course it's new and so it's a little bit exciting and a little bit scary, both together. That's what those feelings in your tummy are saying. They mean you're gearing up for something new and we should help you cope.' Mum suggests re-reading the book the school gave them describing what will happen on the first day to reassure and prepare Ivan. Then the whole family plays Ivan's favourite card game until bedtime to help him relax.

Despite the evolutionary argument for the importance of emotion, the Western philosophical tradition has tended to regard emotions as an inconvenience and as vastly inferior to reason. Emotions have been viewed as unpredictable and often damaging – closely allied to sin. The ideal, in this tradition, has been to keep emotion strictly controlled, and often suppressed, and to concentrate on developing reasoning abilities. While some recent changes in these attitudes can be discerned, this is essentially the heritage that has shaped British society (the tradition of the 'stiff upper lip'). It is a heritage that leaves its imprint on how parents bring up their children and on our education system.

Reflection 5.1

- Consider the attitudes to emotion in your own upbringing. Would you describe your family as emotional? Were emotions discussed? Were some emotions 'swept under the carpet'? Were there gender differences in the messages given to boys and girls regarding the emotions it was permissible to display?
- Try to think of a specific incident in your childhood that captures key aspects of your family's emotional approach.
- What sort of attitudes to emotion are you modelling for children? To what extent are these attitudes a reflection of your own upbringing? Or have you consciously chosen to adopt a different attitude to emotions?
- What sort of behaviours do you think indicate emotionality? Is there always a direct relationship between emotion and behaviour? What do you feel about the recent trend for more overt embracing and saying 'Love you'? To what extent do you consider this a good thing? Is it sometimes superficial and habitual?

Emotions: a help or hindrance in life today?

Goleman (1996) popularised the term 'emotional intelligence' which usefully focuses attention on the role of emotional and social functioning – not just intellectual functioning – in life satisfaction and success. Emotions provide us with a way of coping with the infinite amount of perceptual material that bombards us and they, and their close relation, intuition, prioritise what we notice and remember. They also direct our actions, our behaviour. They play a role in babies' lives from the very beginning (see Box 5.1).

Box 5.1: Emotions and development

Basic emotions

Most textbooks assert that there are six basic emotions and that babies of any culture will show the facial expressions for these by the time they are 7 months old. The six basic emotions are considered to be: happiness, sadness, anger, disgust, surprise and fear.

Recent work (Jack et al. 2014) suggests that there may be only four basic emotions: happiness, sadness, 'approach and deal with' (which within the first year separates into anger and disgust) and 'avoid' (which within the first year separates into surprise and fear).

Later-appearing emotions

These later-appearing emotions evident by 24 months are: shame, guilt, jealousy, embarrassment and pride.

While the ability to reflect on others' emotions and consider them explicitly develops significantly with age, research suggests that babies are responsive to others' emotions, and the emotional climate, from birth. Emotion is communicated in myriad ways, including touch, tone of voice and facial expression. The baby's early understanding of emotion is 'interactive' rather than 'abstracted' (Reddy 2008: 79). In the context of engaged interaction, a 2-month-old responds to emotional cues.

Positive emotions have the same role now as in our evolutionary history. They power the virtuous cycle of positive relationships within which people can flourish. This has been discussed in detail with regard to attachment theory and its implications, including children's need to feel special, noticed and valued in settings. Positive interactions and emotions are what makes or breaks relationships. Seligman (2011: 48), looking at adult relationships, points out that 'how you celebrate is more predictive of strong relations than how you fight'. Having arguments may at times be healthy for relationships but what is absolutely vital is having positive times together. Seligman argues that an approach to helping people that focuses on minimising problems (for example, helping a child to find coping strategies for anger) is limited. For people to flourish, it is essential also to build strong relationships, feelings of happiness, enjoyment, belonging and achievement. The focus should not just be on addressing perceived problems but on fostering the positive emotions as well, working to try to make these predominate in a child's experience. This must be borne in mind for children whose behaviour is considered challenging. At least as much effort should go into building positive relationships and eliciting positive emotions as goes into addressing the challenging behaviour, not least because the strategies to address unwanted behaviour will work only if the child has a relationship and the attendant desire to (re-)establish goodwill with the adult.

Are the 'negative' emotions of value in life today? Now that most of us do not face life-or-death situations every day, are the negative emotions such as anger more of a hindrance than a help? It is quick, intuitive, emotion-driven behaviours, such as angry outbursts of violence, which have resulted in emotion often being considered dangerous and unfortunate. An example of quick emotion-driven behaviour is John Prescott's reaction to having eggs thrown at him on a visit to Rhyl in 2001. Prescott, then Deputy Prime Minister, lashed out at his assailant. This was not a statesman-like way to behave (though, interestingly, Prescott's image suffered no serious damage as a result). It is open to debate whether this behaviour was functional (helpful) for Prescott (did it deter others from pelting him with eggs?). Emotions work functionally for most people, most of the time and without them we would be unable to function quickly and efficiently. Reasoning takes time. It is a very useful adjunct to emotion but not a replacement. Emotions lead to primary appraisals – 'gut instincts' – that are our inbuilt reactions to stimuli. The negative emotions indicate that something is wrong and needs to be addressed if well-being is to be maintained. We are more dependent on our 'quick and dirty' emotional reactions than we generally realise. Many drivers can think of occasions where they have intuitively taken action to avoid a car accident, and their body is flooded with the fear response, long before their conscious mind has even registered the danger, let alone worked out what to do about it. Our emotions and intuitions often work below the level of consciousness and, generally, are like silent guardian angels, acting to help us thrive. As long as we develop the **executive functions** (the subject of Chapter 9) to enable us to harness our emotions when appropriate, they are some of our best tools for autonomy and well-being.

Understanding the negative emotions may play a particularly important role in the development of autonomy (Lagattuta and Wellman 2001; Hughes and Dunn 2002; Ensor and Hughes 2005). Recognising the whispers (first signs) of negative emotions and acting on them before they have to shout (stage an emotional hijack) may be key in achieving the healthy autonomy that also preserves relationships.

Gottman provides useful guidance on helping children understand the whispers of behaviour (Gottman et al. 1996; Gottman with Declaire 1997). He has identified an aspect of parenting which he believes to be highly influential for children's behaviour and which he describes as being somewhat different from both the responsive style of parenting associated with secure attachment (Ainsworth and Bell 1970; Ainsworth and Marvin 1995) and the authoritative parenting style (Baumrind 1966) associated with best outcomes. Gottman et al. (1996) conducted a study investigating the links between what they termed 'parental **meta-emotion philosophy**' and their children's behaviour. The researchers looked at how parents' feelings and thoughts about emotion (their 'meta-emotion philosophy') affected how they interacted with their children. Some parents were dismissive of their own and children's negative emotions, ignoring or denying these emotions and seeking to distract children on to something else or telling them off for negative emotions. It was not that these parents did not love their children, but they had trouble with negative emotions. The following would be the sorts of comment such parents might make to their children:

> Of course you don't hate your brother.
> Never mind that Layla won't let you play, you have plenty of other friends.
> You are such a lucky boy compared to so many other children. I don't want to hear another word about the weather ruining our plans.
> Don't be angry with me. I've been really busy at work all day and the comic shop was closed by the time I got there.
> Pets do die, I'm afraid. We'll choose a new kitten this weekend.
> I won't have jealousy in this house.

This style of interacting with children is common but it undermines autonomy. Children are effectively being told how they should feel and that it is wrong to have the emotions they experience. Instead of learning adaptive ways of acknowledging and reacting to their emotions, they may be learning that they have to hide parts of themselves to be accepted. Emotions that are driven underground spell trouble for the future. They can interfere with the quality of relationships and cause simmering resentment or frustration. Autonomy is not fostered when feelings are denied.

Contrasting with this approach, Gottman's team identified an 'emotion coaching' style of parenting. Parents using this style value negative emotions as well as positive ones. They encourage children to tune into all their emotions and help them to label and understand them. These parents do not put limits on emotions but will, if necessary, put boundaries on behaviour. The message they give their children is 'It is alright to feel angry/sad/jealous or any emotion at all but it is not alright to hurt anyone because of these feelings'. The emotion-coaching parent listens to the child, gives some time for the emotion to hold sway and then, at an appropriate point, asks questions designed to prompt the child towards effective problem solving.

Gottman et al. (1996) reported on a longitudinal study carried out with 56 families, when their children were 4–5 years old and again when they were 8 years old. A host of measures was taken, including semi-structured interviews with both parents and children, teacher ratings of aggression towards peers, naturalistic observations and laboratory observations where parents had to ask children about a story that had just been told and then to teach the child to play a game. Physiological measurements of the child's vagal tone in different circumstances (thought to relate to the child's emotional regulation) were taken and the child's general health was monitored. From all this data, the researchers explored a range of models to account for the children's long-term progress. The five steps of the Emotion Coaching programme represent the practical application of what the research suggested resulted in the best outcomes for the children in terms of their physical and mental health, their positive behaviour and their social popularity and academic achievement. The five steps (Gottman with Declaire 1997: 75) are:

1   *Being aware of the child's emotion.* Children may be unable or unwilling to say what is bothering them and sometimes adults find it hard to work it out. Remember that we cannot always fully account for our own feelings. You might want to hazard a guess about a child's feelings but do so tentatively and do not bombard the child with your own ideas. Sometimes you might have to be patient and do some detective work to formulate a hypothesis about how a child feels. Listening and thinking are often more valuable than talking.

2   *Recognising the emotion as an opportunity for intimacy and teaching.* Remember that spending the time to understand a child and support them with the whispers of emotions saves the shouts. This is preventative work. Try not to brush aside issues that seem to you minor in the scale of things. It is by grasping the autonomy-supporting opportunities that arise naturally that you best help children.

3   *Listening empathetically and validating the child's feelings.* 'Nice' people want to help. There is a very strong urge for them to jump in and solve problems for others. Instead, listen carefully and just make interested or supportive noises. Your role is to help the child understand emotions and then come up with ways forward. You are coaching, not doing it for the child. Slow down and fight the temptation to take immediate control and make everything alright.

4   *Helping the child verbally label emotions.* You have the vocabulary and the language skills to support the child's learning. Remember that people often have mixed feelings and it is important to acknowledge this.

5   *Setting limits while helping the child problem-solve.* Limits must be set on behaviour. This is the 'it's fine to experience uncomfortable feelings but it is definitely not fine to hurt anyone' part of emotion coaching.

Sometimes it will also be appropriate to set limits on the rumination over negative feelings. Airing and acknowledging feelings are healthy, ruminating over them is not. Problem-solving can encompass things children might do to put a situation right and things to try to avoid a similar situation in the future. It can also include helpful ways to 'release' feelings and limit rumination, such as physical activities, listening to music or engaging in an enjoyable, engrossing activity. Adults should try to prompt the child towards solutions to problems, rather than imposing their own ideas.

Recent work in the UK using emotion coaching in settings and schools is producing promising results and indicates that children, practitioners and parents find the approach helpful (Rose et al. 2012).

Case snippet 5.2: Saheed

Saheed is a 6-year-old with a quick temper. He has a twin, Amir, whom he frequently hits and kicks, both in school and at home. His parents and school staff tell him off when they see this behaviour. The effect has not been to stop the behaviour but to drive it underground. Saheed is ever sneakier with his hitting and kicking but Amir's bruises suggest they are happening just as often. Finally, the school refers Saheed for work with a teaching assistant who is trained to support children with social, emotional and behavioural difficulties. She builds up a relationship with Saheed and the family, chats with him and observes him in different situations. She realises that Saheed may be jealous of his twin. Based on this insight, she is able to help Saheed's family and the teacher come up with various strategies to help him. In her work with Saheed, she helps him explore jealousy. Her approach is not to tell Saheed that he does not feel jealous or that he has no cause for jealousy. Instead, she works on his reaction to it. She encourages him to take it as signal that he needs to take action to feel more comfortable within himself and within his family. She helps him (and his family) look at situations where he does not feel jealous and to analyse why this is and how such situations might be extended. They look together at whether there are any particular barriers to Saheed's well-being that he could overcome with help. He says he cannot read as well as Amir and agrees to some reading time being incorporated into his sessions with the assistant. They also look at activities that he thinks he would enjoy and it is agreed that Saheed can join a karate class whereas Amir will choose a different extracurricular activity. The approach that proves successful for Saheed derives from recognising his biologically programmed jealousy rather than denying it. It enables him to accept and build an identity that is different from his twin. Both these factors are important in enabling Saheed to develop autonomy.

Key points

- Emotions are part of what makes us human and from birth babies are sensitive to the emotional tone around them.
- Emotions serve purposes and denying them is unhealthy and impedes development of autonomy.
- Positive emotions support relationships, learning and creativity. Having fun with children is one of the most fruitful things parents, practitioners and teachers can do.
- If children's behaviour is a cause for concern, try to build up their positive experiences in addition to tackling the behaviour.
- Promote positive behaviour by helping children to learn to use negative emotions as an early warning system so that their behaviour is not emotionally hijacked.
- The five steps of 'emotion coaching' (Gottman with Declaire 1997) provide a useful practical framework for supporting children's emotional understanding.

Further reading

Early Education supported by the Department for Education (2012) *Development Matters in the Early Years Foundation Stage (EYFS)*, London: Early Education.
Practitioners might wish to reinforce the messages in this chapter by looking through the PSE sections of *Development Matters* and noting the guidance on the development of emotions.

Faber, A. and Mazlish, E. (1980) *How to Talk so Kids Will Listen and Listen so Kids Will Talk*, New York: Avon Books.
Gottman, J. with Declaire, J. (1997) *The Heart of Parenting: How to Raise an Emotionally Intelligent Child*, London: Bloomsbury.
Both the books listed above are full of wonderful examples to guide adults with an emotion coaching approach. These authors were all students of Dr Haim Ginott whose influence shines through in their work.

Oatley, K., Keltner, D. and Jenkins, J.M. (2006) *Understanding Emotions*, 2nd edn, Oxford: Blackwell.
This large textbook provides a wealth of information on all aspects of emotions and emotional development.

6

Unique but belonging
'I want to be me but I still need to be loved'

Discovering difference

Toddlers are busy little learners. They generally take great delight in their increasing accomplishments. Walking confidently, running, climbing, reaching for things, exploring – these can be heady pleasures. Falling and hurting themselves, being stopped from doing what they want – these unleash distress and frustration. Many toddlers live on an emotional rollercoaster, they are particularly passionate little people. In their second year, children usually delight in doing things on their own, a sign of burgeoning autonomy. Less endearing for the adults supporting them, but equally a sign of developing autonomy, is toddlers' tendency to resist being helped. Hair washing, nappy changing and other necessary tasks which the younger baby co-operated with may now become battlegrounds (see Box 6.1). Toddlerhood is when children start to realise that their wants and desires may clash with those of other people. They are at the beginning of a long learning project – how to balance individuality with social acceptance, how to do their own thing but retain the benefits of belonging.

Adults can do much to promote positive behaviour if they understand the range of behaviour typical for this age group and adopt autonomy-supporting approaches, maintaining warm relationships through the struggles that developing autonomy may entail (see Box 6.1). Readers can remind themselves of the principles of autonomy supporting environments by looking back at the introduction to Part 2.

Box 6.1: Autonomy-granting support for necessary tasks

- 'Let's get these toys off the floor. Granny could easily trip over them and fall' (giving a reason).
- 'Shall I put the shampoo on your hand to rub in or do you want me to do it? Shall I hold the flannel over your eyes or will you?' (offering limited choice).

- 'You're tired and just want to sleep. We need to get you washed and changed. Let's do it as quickly as possible. Can you make it easy for me to help you? Will it help if I sing? (acknowledging feelings).
- 'The cars are all like Chitty Chitty Bang Bang. They can fly into the cupboard' (making a game, appealing to the child's interest).
- 'Right we need boots, coats and hats on to go to the shop. You decide the order to put them on' (choice of sequencing).
- 'Brushing those teeth up and down, top teeth and bottom teeth. Keep your smile bright and white, like the dentist said' (giving reason).
- 'We'll all need warm sweaters for later because it's going to be cold. Which do you want to pack – your red or the blue?' (limited choice).
- 'It stings when I clean your cut? Poor you. I need to do it so it gets better quickly' (acknowledging feeling/giving reason).

Clashes are part of typical development

The developmental pattern of 'tantrums' in toddlers is both anecdotally well known and documented in research (see Box 6.2). Dunn (1988) (see Box 6.3) found that toddlers aged 14–24 months old complied with their mother's requests at a consistent rate (on average nine times in each two-hour period of observation). However, the number of compliances remained the same throughout, what changed in a later part of this age range was a *doubling* of the frequency with which toddlers argued with their mother, ignored her demands or did exactly what they were told not to do. How might we understand this behaviour in toddlers? As babies, they had enjoyed influencing adults by drawing them into smiling and positive exchanges. Now the toddler and adult are often engaged in a battle of wills. Toddlers' strong exploratory drive, coupled with their increasing physical abilities to get around, result in boundaries being tested. Self-awareness is developing apace as children differentiate between themselves and others. They discover that people have different feelings and opinions about the same things. This is the foundation on which the sense of autonomy will be built.

Box 6.2: The 'doing it my way' part of trying to become autonomous

What does research tell us about typical behaviours in the early years?

Aggression
- Only 28 per cent of toddlers show little or no aggression.
- At 17 months, most children display aggression towards adults, siblings and peers.

(Continued)

- Most of these show slightly increasing aggression over the period until they are 3½ years old. Their levels of aggression then drop before they are 5 years old.
- 14 per cent of children become much more aggressive over the same period and these are the children at serious risk of long-term problems and poor outcomes (Tremblay et al. 2004).
- 2- and 3-year-olds used coercive methods in 91 per cent of clashes in childcare settings, and in 42 per cent of cases this was physical aggression (Singer and de Haan 2007).

Resisting parents' demands
- Children's resistance to their mother's demands *doubled* between the ages of 18 and 24 months. Resistance included ignoring, arguing and carrying out forbidden behaviours (Dunn 1988).
- Defiance in the second year is not correlated with defiance at age 4. Defiance usually declines from age 24–30 months onwards (Kuczynski and Kochanska 1990).
- Defiance towards parents from 30–60 months is correlated with poor social competence and poor relationship with parents (Kochanska 2002).

The study often cited as illustrative of children's recognition that people do not have the same likes and dislikes is the cracker and broccoli experiment (Gopnik et al. 2001: 36). The vast majority of babies and toddlers prefer crackers to broccoli. In the experiment they see adults, some of whom show a strong preference for crackers and others for broccoli. The test is whether the children will offer broccoli to those adults who showed this preference or whether they will nevertheless offer these adults the crackers which they themselves prefer. Fourteen-month-olds offer adults the cracker regardless of the preference shown by the adult whereas 18-month-olds can offer broccoli appropriately. This shows that 18-month-old children can grasp that people have different desires.

One interpretation of the battles of toddlerhood is that toddlers are fascinated by the discovery of differences in attitudes and feelings and are driven to work out as much as they can about people's reactions (Gopnik et al. 2001). The resultant clashes raise further issues of engrossing interest: the limits of their power. At the same time, toddlers' still immature language comprehension means that often they keep pushing for what they want (e.g. wailing for a biscuit) rather than being pacified by a verbal promise ('You'll get one after I've finished the ironing'). These interpretations encompass some of the behaviour familiar to parents and practitioners and corroborated by research, such as the tendency of toddlers to look directly at the adult, sometimes laughing, when continuing to do something that has been forbidden (it is the adult's reaction that is of interest and produces the excitement) (Gopnik et al. 2001). But conflicts are 'relational work'

(Singer and de Haan 2007) on two fronts. Not only are toddlers very interested in other people's reactions but, despite initiating or prolonging conflicts, they usually want to restore close relations with the important people in their lives. Relatedness is important and can help both child and adult recover from some of the 'fireworks' of behaviour typical of this period. Toddlers often cry and seek hugs and reassurance after conflicts that they themselves have escalated. This is a healthy sign.

Case snippet 6.1: Lola

Lola, 2 years old, loves the range of activities at nursery and particularly enjoys playing outside. Kate, her Key Person, knows that Lola is aware of the rules regarding turn-taking because they discussed them in a small group yesterday and Lola was the one who said, 'Your turn on the tricycle is over when the red flag is waved'. This morning Lola was on the tricycle and ignored the red flag. Kate knows she saw it but even when she went right over to Lola, waving the flag, Lola turned her head away and cycled off. Kate had to raise her voice to get Lola to hand the tricycle to Nathan. She calmly reminded Lola of the rule. Ten minutes later, however, Lola had secured another go and again reacted to the flag by heading off in the opposite direction. Kate ran after her and told her very firmly to give up the tricycle. Lola stared at her and for a split second Kate thought she was going to refuse. Lola jumped off the tricycle, dissolved into tears, sobbing, 'Sorry, sorry, sorry.' Kate knelt down to Lola's level, hugging and reassuring her.

Difference as an opportunity to support autonomy

The research data on the occurrence of aggressive and defiant behaviour of many toddlers (see Box 6.2) supports a view that such behaviour is a typical developmental pattern in children aged from approximately 1 year old up until $3\frac{1}{2}$ years old. Dix et al. (2007), in a study involving parents and children aged 14–27 months, found that some parents who were attuned to their children and used autonomy-granting controls had children who complied willingly. Others, with the same parenting approaches, had children who at this stage were defiant and resisted demands. They suggest that some 'defiance' at this stage can be interpreted as children feeling safe enough to try to exert autonomy but doing so in a clumsy way. Similarly, Maccoby (1980: 149) argues that some aggression shown by one young child to another can be interpreted as a form of developing autonomy and as more mature than seeking adult support or 'giving in', while clearly less mature than negotiation and compromise. Maccoby (1980: 126) also suggests that in the toddler and early pre-school period, the most sociable children engage in the greatest amount of both positive and negative behaviours, with positive behaviours coming to the fore by the time of school entry. In the Dix et al. study (2007), the defiant children in warm relationships with their parents made many positive overtures to their parents quite separate from their defiant behaviour. These findings and ideas suggest that for many children crucial learning takes place through conflict in the toddler and early pre-school period. Most of them internalise social demands and can avoid or handle much conflict without aggression by the time they enter school. The persistence of a high level of aggressive and defiant behaviour at school entry is less typical and much more worrying because it is associated with poorer behavioural and other outcomes over the long term. This developmental pattern is associated with lack of warmth between parent and child and with lack of engagement with others in co-operative play.

Box 6.3: Judy Dunn (1939–): longitudinal, naturalistic studies of children's relationships and social and emotional development

Judy Dunn, professor at King's College, London, is well known for her naturalistic studies of children and families at home. Just as Mary Ainsworth carried out naturalistic studies of mothers and babies, throwing light on attachment, Judy Dunn studied families at home and provided a wealth of valuable detail about children's social and emotional development. In her seminal Cambridge studies, she and her colleagues tracked the development of over 50 children and their families by observing and audiotaping them in their homes for two-hour periods at intervals when the second-born children were aged 1–3 years old. Observations were systematic, with a running record made every ten seconds and behaviour later categorised and coded.

Dunn (1988) tracked how mothers naturally altered their response to their children as the children's abilities increased. Maternal responses to crying reduced after the first year but this was balanced by mothers became increasingly responsive to their children's attempts to use language during the second year. She noted that mothers increasingly mentioned mental states (feelings, beliefs, thoughts, motivations) in their conversation with their second-born children when these children were aged 13–18 months. The children began commenting on people's mental states at about 18 months and at the same period, mothers were referring to people's feelings, the consequences of actions and socially acceptable behaviour in 33 per cent of instances of conflict. As the children's language and understanding developed, their mothers talked about 'mental states' and their relation to behaviour even more often – in just over half of the instances of conflict when the children were 2 years old. Dunn argues that the mothers were not just responding to children but also *shaping* their social understanding, helping them develop autonomy: 'Conversational analyses reveal that children are growing up in a world in which rules are clearly and continually articulated for them, at a level that matches their own changing abilities' (Dunn 1988: 38).The dialogue on the clashes of will that toddlers encounter is crucial teaching that in most cases enables children over time to develop ways of managing their emotions and accommodating their behaviour to others and to the social expectations within the family.

What can adults do to promote children's learning over what can be a period of conflict? The importance of establishing and maintaining reasonable boundaries was discussed in Chapter 4. The manner in which adults respond to conflicts is important. Autonomy-granting approaches need to be employed within the context of strong relationships and mutual respect. Adults should aim to be calm but firm and to remember that young children need support, guidance and repetition to learn. **Inductive socialisation** practices (see Box 6.4) are believed to be helpful. This refers to providing behavioural guidance with explanation and reasoning. There is also a great deal of evidence for the benefits of tuning children into others' perspectives and feelings. Adult use of '**mental state' talk** (talk about what people feel, think, know, remember and believe) is associated with children's development of '**Theory of Mind**' (understanding of people's differing viewpoints) (Dunn et al. 1991; Ensor and Hughes 2005; Harris et al. 2005; Harris 2006). As children develop this understanding of other people's emotional lives, and provided they are in a context of warm relationships, they are likely to behave in a positive and autonomous fashion (Ensor and Hughes 2005). Inductive approaches foster empathy and are associated with self-determined autonomy. Contrasting approaches such as punishment and threat result in children focusing on external consequences that will affect them. The result is more likely to be controlled autonomy (Krevans and Gibbs 1996), outward behaviour that conforms to social expectations but which is not fulfilling the child's psychological needs and so increases the risk of later behaviour or psychological problems.

Box 6.4: Adult reaction to conflict: inductive discipline

It is sensible to accord with children's language levels when addressing behaviour.

For the youngest children, keep information simple:

No biting! That hurts.
No hitting! You've hurt Ella – she's crying.

(Continued)

With children's increasing understanding, more information can be given:

You want to play with the ball? But Billy was playing with it – you've interrupted his game and he's upset. It's not fair just to grab. Give Billy the ball back. Now, how could you get to play with the ball? (prompting solutions encourages a child to rehearse words for asking to join in or for asking to have the next turn).

Kara was in your way but you can't just push her out of the way. Look, she got a shock and she knocked her arm and it's hurting. What should you do? (prompts apology). Remember to ask people nicely if they can move. What could you say? (encourages a child to rehearse a request to move).

Children who are hurt or have their rights infringed by others should be encouraged to voice their feelings to the child concerned. ('That hurt!', 'I was playing with that. It makes me cross that you grabbed it away. Give it back', 'Hey, I was playing with Luke. It makes me angry that you're taking him away and not letting me play too.')

Helping children to be assertive without retaliating physically is a key skill for autonomy but one that is likely to need practice.

The level of induction and mental state talk used in sorting out conflicts will vary according to the age and understanding of the children. Box 6.4 gives an outline of the approach. Conflicts provide excellent opportunities for training in negotiation. Adults should model negotiation in adult-to-adult differences of opinion and in clashes with children. Part of the authoritative style (see Chapter 4) involves some flexibility on less important aspects of what the adult decrees, whilst remaining firm on the important points. If parents need to hurry out with a child and tell her to get ready quickly and leave all her toys behind, but she argues to bring lots of toys with her, they might, for example, agree that she can choose one toy to bring as long as she is ready soon. Many young children quickly grasp the idea of negotiating with their parents and become rather inventive and adopt a 'bargaining' approach in their attempts. Adults need to be patient and to avoid letting a power struggle develop as the conversations can be rich learning experiences for children. Some teachers, however, react badly to children's attempts to negotiate with them. Parents of keen little negotiators may need to prepare their children for the fact that there can be different expectations of compliance in different places, but equally teachers of young children may need to reflect on how group settings do not always have practices that encourage fledgling autonomy.

Children's disputes with one another may be hotspots for learning the skills of negotiation. Adults should avoid intervening too early if no one is in danger of being physically hurt. Children learn from settling their own disputes. Singer and de Haan found that 79 per cent of disputes they observed in group settings were settled without adult involvement. (Some minor disputes were not noticed by the adults in charge.) There will, however, be times where adult intervention is necessary and coaching in negotiation is helpful. Box 6.5 outlines the process.

Box 6.5: Helping children in conflict to negotiate

- Calm the children first. They may not be ready to enter into discussion until intense emotions have subsided.
- Ascertain what happened from each child's viewpoint – avoid questions such as 'Why did you hit him?' Instead ask more open questions, such as 'Alfie, tell me what happened' (some children will find this too open and you might need to make guesses – phrase them tentatively so that children are free to correct your interpretation: 'Alfie, did you want a turn on the bike?').
- Try to limit dispute over the details. Encourage each child to give an account that reveals what they want now as well as what happened. Try not to jump to conclusions and assume one child is to blame.
- Give clear messages about the unacceptability of any behaviour that hurt others or damaged property. 'Mia, hitting is never the right way to go about things. You need to say sorry to Alfie for hurting him.' You may also need to tackle any behaviour that provoked the unacceptable behaviour. 'Alfie, Mia shouldn't have hit you and she has said sorry but it wouldn't have happened if you hadn't stopped her riding the bike. That's what made her angry. What do you think you should do?' (prompt apology and/or offer to let her back on the bike).
- Ask children for solutions: 'So, is there any way you can both get what you want? Is there anything you can do to feel happier with each other?' Children who are close friends are more likely to find ways to play together after disputes (Dunn 2004; Singer and de Haan 2007). It is not necessary that children should always do so.

Licht et al. (2008) report some research based on observing children in day-care centres in Switzerland when they were 8, 14 and 22 months old. They noted that the majority of conflicts between young children were driven by one child's desire to continue an activity when another child was curious to use the same equipment or toy. The researchers classified the motivations behind such conflicts as 'interrupted activity' or 'exploration'. Children wanted to play with toys and the other child was an obstacle to this but the focus was on playing with the toy, not on a 'mine' versus 'yours' dispute with attendant emotions regarding the other child. Anger was not seen in incidents classified this way. Only at 22 months were conflicts observed that were classified as 'possession' disputes, with children more interested in possessing the object, getting or keeping it away from another, than in playing with it. Also at this age, some conflicts classified as motivated by 'dominance' began to appear. These too were emotionally intense. The child did not necessarily want the object but wanted to control what was done by the object – to make the other child carry out the requisite action. Children exerting their power over one another in this way is probably more common than practitioners and teachers realise (Singer and de Haan 2007; Grieshaber and McArdle 2010). Such disputes are common among siblings too. Even more unfortunately, some adults enter into power disputes with children (Dreikurs et al. 1971). In addition to dealing with disputes as they arise, using the approaches already outlined, it may be important to check whether more could be done to enable those 'abusing' their power to feel more secure and valued as unique individuals (an important part of autonomy). Can anything be done to strengthen their relationships? Have they wide and appropriately challenging opportunities for competence? Can older and physically stronger children be given responsibilities in relation to younger and less strong children (Singer and de Haan 2007)? If a child seems to want to dominate, the adult might play with the child, giving the child a chance to take the powerful role while s/he assumes the less powerful role (for example, adult as baby or pupil?) (Singer and de Haan 2007). Siblings often vie for parents' attention and interest, and this can be particularly the case if they are the same gender and close in age (or 'multiples' – the same age). There can be a need to help children forge a positive identity, authentic to themselves and not just formed in reaction to siblings (whether in imitation or as a complete contrast to a sibling.) 'Emotion coaching' (Chapter 5) is one aspect of support. Part 3 (Competence) provides some additional pointers.

Other ways of developing autonomy-supporting communication skills

While the clashes of toddlerhood and childhood provide opportunities for children to understand other perspectives and to learn to negotiate, they are far from the only ways that children learn these valuable skills. Some children rarely have disputes with others but acquire excellent understanding of others and advanced negotiation skills. Such children's behaviour is unlikely to cause concern. It is worth briefly considering some of the other means by which children learn about themselves and others as maximising the relevant opportunities could benefit all children.

'Mental state' talk in general conversation and in discussion of events and stories is important. Emotion coaching (Chapter 5) is rich in such talk. Analyses of naturally occurring conversation show that families differ significantly in the amount of such talk, which achieves the same purpose as inductive discipline, sensitising children to others' feelings, thought and motivations. Dunn et al. (1991) found that 3-year-olds who at home experienced more discussion of emotions and motivations showed a greater understanding of others' perspectives when aged 6 than did children exposed to less of this type of conversation. Experiments have shown that exposing children to 'mental state' language significantly improved their ability to understand others' viewpoints, compared with children in a control group (Harris et al. 2005). As noted in Chapter 5, discussion of 'negative' emotions (anger, jealousy, and so on) is thought to be particularly important (Lagattuta and Wellman 2001; Hughes and Dunn 2002; Ensor and Hughes 2005). Staff in settings can usefully promote these conversations. MacLure et al. (2012) warn about the importance of maintaining authenticity when doing so. Too formulaic, exaggerated or stereotyped an approach may be unhelpful.

Box 6.6: 'Mental state' talk

- 'Emily's watching you. She'd like to be your friend. She'll be happy if you let her dress up.'
- 'Daddy will be pleased if you're in bed, ready for him to read to you.'
- 'Jamie's excited, he's looking forward to the party.'
- 'Mummy is very tired and a bit sad because her friend is upset. That was what the long phone call was about.'
- 'I know you don't like having your bath but Harry enjoys his. He likes having bubble bath and giving himself a white beard.'
- 'Daddy was expecting an important letter today and it hasn't come, that's why he is grumpy'.
- 'Let's think. Where do you think my car keys could be? We need to remember the last time we used the car and what we did when we got in.'
- 'Jamie's scared because he got jam on the library book and he thinks his teacher will be cross.''
- 'Granny was worried because we didn't phone when we got in last night. People like to be reassured that everything is OK – like when I come in to see you after Daddy and I go out at night.'
- 'Hey – here's a surprise – the postman delivered this parcel for you.'
- 'It's disappointing that it's raining. It means we can't have the picnic or if we do, we'll get very wet!'
- 'Sam's frowning because she's thinking very hard about her homework. She's concentrating. She's not cross.'
- 'Why are you smiling? It's not funny! Oh, do you know where the chocolate is? Did you play a trick on me?'

Task 6.1

Listen to conversation in your setting/home for a few short periods over a day. Listen also to the discussion when a book is shared. How much 'mental state' talk occurs? (See Box 6.6.) Are there missed opportunities for 'mental state' talk? Is the relevant talk authentic?

Children engaging with each other in pretend play provide a tremendously valuable context in which they hone their understanding of others and their negotiating skills. Brown et al. (1996) found that 47-month-old children used much more 'mental state' language in pretend play with close friends and with siblings than they did with their parents. Children also showed their strongest abilities to reconcile differing points of view and continue playing together in this context. The significant role of pretend play will be further examined in Part 3. Here we need to note that although adults cannot replicate the experience of pretend play with children, they do have a role in recognising its importance and in valuing children's chosen friendships, providing opportunities and time for extended role play.

Children at risk of missing out on beginning to develop self-determined autonomy in the early years

Engaging with passionate little people as they develop their autonomy can be fascinating and rewarding. Many parents and practitioners enjoy this period of childhood when character emerges so clearly and can be nurtured and shaped in a positive fashion. However, autonomy-supporting approaches are not necessarily what parents themselves experienced or something they know about and whose value they understand. Furthermore, they require considerable emotional resources on the part of adults.

There is, not surprisingly, considerable consistency between the groups who are vulnerable to insecure attachment (see Chapter 3) and those vulnerable to developing controlled as opposed to self-determined autonomy. There are suggestions that children of depressed mothers tend to be passive and non-assertive as toddlers (Dix et al. 2007) and miss typical opportunities to develop autonomy.

There is, as noted in the discussion of authoritarian parenting (Chapter 4) an association between harsh, coercive management styles and challenging behaviour. Earlier in this chapter, the frequency of aggression in many young children was noted and the argument proposed that, for many, it is a sign of the beginnings of autonomy. In these children, levels of aggression fall and prosocial behaviour increases before school age. For a small group (Tremblay et al. 2004), aggression levels rise steeply through the pre-school years and into school, and these children are at risk of ongoing serious behaviour difficulties. This long-term aggression is not self-determined – rather, it is controlled. These children's behaviour is controlled by external factors – they do not experience themselves as the source of their actions, rather they react against demands, constraints and slights (real or perceived). Skinner and Edge (2002) describe this as 'oppositional coping' and stress how the behaviour is reactive and in effect controlled by others, though not in the form those others might desire. Oppositional children and their parents often get locked into mutual coercion (Kochanska et al. 2009), depicted by Porter (2013: 117) as 'the 'dance' of escalating adult coercion and child defiance. In settings and schools also there is a real danger that these children get caught in a vicious cycle of action and reaction that compounds their initial difficulties. Adults who normally adopt autonomy-supporting methods can find themselves becoming more authoritarian in the face of the child's reaction to them. Aggression, when not leavened by prosocial behaviour at other times, often results in peer rejection (Volling et al. 1993). These children may therefore have limited access to join pretend play and other peer activities that might support the development of self-determination (Figure 6.1).

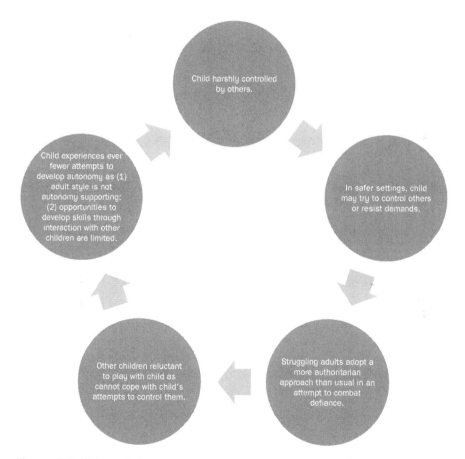

Figure 6.1 Vicious circle when autonomy is harshly undermined

A different but equally vicious cycle could work in the case of children who are rather passive and compliant, whether related to parental depression, over-protection or other reasons (Figure 6.2). Here a passive child complies easily and people do not realise that this comes from copying others or just doing what is expected. Adults do not recognise that the child has not developed a secure and autonomous sense of self and therefore do not provide support, time and

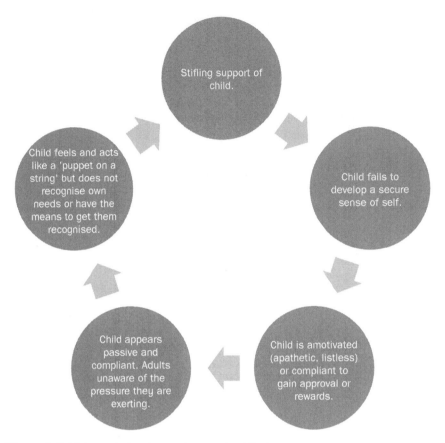

Figure 6.2 Vicious circle when autonomy is stifled

opportunity for this to form. Such children do not face up to stressful situations in an active way, thus missing out on the autonomy-building effects of successful 'coping' (Skinner and Edge 2002).

Key points

- When children delight in doing things for themselves, this is an early sign of autonomy.
- Toddlerhood to school age is a crucial time for establishing the likely long-term pattern of a child's autonomy, whether this is self-determined (healthiest) or controlled (less healthy).
- Toddlers start to realise differences between their desires and those of others. How adults handle the resultant clashes is important for the form of autonomy that develops.

- In the home situation, children under about $2\frac{1}{2}$ years old who resist help, object to normal care routines and defy their parents' requests may be showing normal early signs of developing autonomy. This is particularly the case if they want to be cuddled and comforted by parents after major disputes and if they generally have a warm relationship.
- Physical aggression is common among $1-3\frac{1}{2}$-year-olds, including aggression between young children in group settings.
- Using incidents as opportunities to help children understand the perspectives of others is helpful, as is general 'mental state' talk in the course of everyday events and sharing books.
- Autonomy-granting support treats children respectfully, recognising feelings and offering reasons and limited choices.
- It is helpful to model and support children with acceptable ways of achieving their ends, such as ways of joining in, ways of negotiating, ways of apologising or making amends.
- Overprotection and intrusive helpfulness can be coercive and inhibit autonomy.
- Quiet, compliant children who copy others or who always do what is expected of them merit further consideration. Check that they can express their feelings, preferences and opinions and gradually support them in doing so, if necessary.
- Value pretend play as a vital context for children to learn about expressing their own needs while taking others' perspectives on board.

Further reading

Gopnik, A., Meltzoff, A. and Kuhl, P. (2001) *How Babies Think*, London: Orion.
Whitebread, D. (2012) *Developmental Psychology and Early Childhood Education*, London: Sage.
These two books, though very different, both present recent research findings in a very readable manner.

Part 3
Competence

'I can'

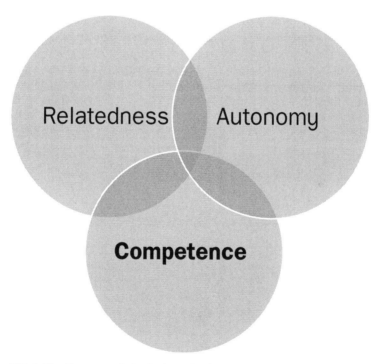

Figure P3.1 The three psychological needs: focus on competence
Source: Based on Deci and Ryan (2000).

Introduction to Part 3

Competence is the final of the three universal and lifelong needs to be examined. We all acknowledge the value of being competent in a range of spheres. We recognise the privileged position of adults who find an occupation that draws on their strengths and enables them to develop in additional ways. Our education system aims to promote children's learning and abilities – to develop their competence.

Unfortunately we also know that many of the children who were eager to learn as toddlers and young children lose their inquisitiveness and thirst for knowledge at some stage. Many sadly do not achieve levels of competence commensurate with the long years they spend in the education system. Some find alternative paths to attaining and feeling competent; others do not.

In self-determination theory (Deci and Ryan 2000, 2002), the interest is in developing a continuing love of learning and belief in one's competence. As in the earlier parts of the book, we will again begin with a list of bullet points which summarises (adult) competence as portrayed in self-determination theory. This will provide the context for our consideration of how to foster the natural inclination towards competence in children and how to avoid practices, often well-intentioned, which undermine competence in the longer term.

Competent individuals

- Feel capable of having an effect on the physical and social environments and attaining valued outcomes.
- Enjoy engaging in interesting activities and exercising all their capacities. They grow and develop a bedrock of competence through doing so.
- Respond positively to novelty and also to setbacks and challenges.
- Are motivated to carry out less interesting but important activities and tasks.

Competence is not

- Only doing things where you are confident of quick success.
- Being brilliant at everything you do.

Competence-supporting environments

- Model a learning approach.
- Have structure – are responsive, predictable, contingent and consistent.

- Place value on people following their interests.
- Provide optimal challenge.
- Enable the development of prerequisite skills.
- Enable the development of fluency, so that skills become predispositions.
- Provide informational feedback.
- Are empathetic to feelings at different points of the learning journey, celebrating effort and strategy as well as achievement.

Environments that undermine competence: harsh

- Model extreme concern with being the best/getting things right.
- May be chaotic and unpredictable.
- Do not value opportunities for people to do activities that interest them.
- Focus exclusively on activities required for external reasons.
- Pose challenges that are well beyond people's capabilities.
- Do not recognise that prerequisite skills need to be developed.
- Offer no opportunities for developing fluency but increase demands very quickly.
- Provide negative feedback.
- Make no acknowledgement of people's feelings.

Environments that undermine competence: smothering

- Model that 'the competent' do things for 'the incompetent'.
- Are over-protective – people are not given the opportunity to experience for themselves the structure and predictability of the environment.
- Only expose people to activities that are easy for them.
- Provide comments, that although positive, are non-specific and do not provide useful information.
- May be kindly intentioned but not really open to others' feelings, e.g. frustration.

Environments that undermine competence: lack of aspiration

- Model a helpless, dependent, listless approach.
- May offer a chaotic, unpredictable environment.
- Provide limited activities to engage in, many of them passive.
- Provide lack of feedback or encouragement. May discourage people from putting in effort.

- Assume others share listlessness, not attuned to possible strivings and ambitions.

Reflection P3.1: Feelings of competence

Reflect on the definition of competence given above. Consider to what degree you feel competent. This may vary in different contexts and your feelings of competence are likely to have varied at different times in your life. To what extent have you experienced competence-supporting or competence-undermining environments? Reflect with regard to the following:

- the home you grew up in;
- your education;
- your current living arrangements;
- your workplace.

Competence in the early years

The need to feel competent is one of the three psychological needs. We tend to think of competence in terms of our performance at certain tasks – I might be competent at cooking for a large group or at writing reports, for example, but less competent at doing plumbing or electrical repairs. Competence as defined in self-determination theory, however, has the broader meaning of feeling that one can make an impact on situations or events. Competence includes the social world of interpersonal relationships as well as the physical world. To feel competent, people need not feel skilled at every task or situation that might confront them. Competence also includes feeling that they could apply themselves and develop further competencies or that, when appropriate, they could find other constructive ways of achieving the desired end (such as seeking help from an adult or recruiting specialised help).

Part 3 outlines how the growing child develops a sense of competence and the conditions that foster this. Competence is related to predictability and a feeling of control. Anxiety results from a lack of these factors. Long-term exposure in childhood to conditions that provoke anxiety rather than competence is thought to create or exacerbate the likelihood of developing 'internalised' behaviour issues which inhibit learning and may show in behaviours such as self-harming and panic attacks (Chorpita and Barlow 1998).

In a sense, all learning potentially contributes to competence. Everyone has different strengths and nurturing any sort of strength may contribute to competence. However, particular types of competence (for example, competence in communication and in literacy and numeracy) are especially prized in our society and educational system. Lagging behind in the acquisition of these specific skills tends to pose a particular threat to perceived competence and there is an association with behavioural issues.

Actual skill and perceived competence are not the same. People may be very highly skilled at, for example, a sport but feel incompetent because they are never 'the best' in a cold, highly competitive environment. Someone with objectively lower skill levels might actually feel more competent and autonomous. The section on competence examines the types of interactions and environments that foster a realistic yet positive sense of perceived competence. It outlines general approaches associated with maintaining the willingness to 'have a go' and keep on learning that too many children lose as they grow up.

Competence and relatedness need to work hand in hand to promote positive behaviour. Children need to have the requisite skills and understanding to be able to interact positively with others and to behave in a socially acceptable manner. They also need to have the relationships with others that motivate them to do so. Dunn's research has repeatedly demonstrated that children demonstrate higher levels of prosocial behaviour in warm relationships (Dunn 1988; Cutting and Dunn 2006). Competence on its own does not necessarily promote positive behaviour, for example, some bullies are extremely adept at 'reading' and exploiting social situations (Sutton et al. 1999).

The structure of Part 3 is as follows:

- Chapter 7 – 'How competence develops: "I need to feel that I can make a difference"'. This chapter explains how competence develops in predictable environments where natural contingencies can easily be recognised. Similarities in the types of environments that promote the three psychological needs – or, alternatively, that thwart them – will be apparent. The role of intrinsic motivation in promoting competence is explored, as are ways in which intrinsic motivation is sometimes undermined. The value of a 'growth mindset' for positive behaviour (Dweck 2008) is emphasised.

- Chapter 8 – 'Communication skills and behaviour: "I need to understand and make myself understood"'. In this chapter, the focus is on an area of competence that is argued to be particularly important in promoting positive behaviour, namely, communication skills. Often it will be helpful to include the development of particular communication skills in the plan for an individual child whose behaviour is of concern.

- Chapter 9 – 'Competence and executive functions: "I need the right sort of opportunities and support to practise skills such as paying attention, waiting and managing impulses"'. The final chapter in Part 3 explains executive functions and their key role in behaviour. Research suggests that '**school readiness**' is better addressed through an '**executive functions**' lens and a wide range of activities than by concentrating solely on academic skills.

Competence and the EYFS

Developing children's competence is arguably the main purpose of the EYFS (DfE 2014b) and competence is threaded right through the framework. Box P3.1 picks out some of the major links between the EYFS and competence as discussed in this part of the book.

Box P3.1: Competence and the EYFS

- The overarching principle that 'every child is a unique child, who is constantly learning and can be resilient, capable, confident and self-assured' captures aspects of competence (earlier versions of the EYFS included the phrase 'a competent learner' in this principle).
- Ideas relating to the value of intrinsic motivation (interests), optimum challenge and play feature in the EYFS:
  - 'learning and development opportunities which are planned around the needs and interests of each individual child';
  - 'igniting children's curiosity and enthusiasm for learning';
  - 'plan a challenging and enjoyable experience for each child in all the areas of learning and development';
  - 'Play is essential for children's development, building their confidence as they learn to explore, think about problems, and relate to others. Children learn by leading their own play.'
- The designation of communication and language as a prime area of learning and development can be read as an acknowledgement of the crucial role of this particular aspect of competence. Executive functions are implicit within the guidance for this aspect.
- The characteristics of effective teaching and learning link with developing growth mindsets:
  - Children 'have a go'.
  - They 'keep on trying' if they encounter difficulties.
  - They 'develop strategies for doing things'.

Source: DfE 20146.

7

How competence develops
'I need to feel I can make a difference'

A predictable, controllable environment

Human beings thrive on predictability. Our brains are pattern-spotting machines and we make sense of the world by detecting patterns. Most of us know and can predict the basic structure of our days. A high degree of predictability frees our brains to concentrate our attention and energy on the novel. We thrive on a balance between predictability and novelty, with the balance weighted towards predictability. Not enough predictability leads to anxiety (Chorpita and Barlow 1998) or rigidity and a feeling of being overwhelmed. Not enough novelty leads to boredom and attendant behaviours, such as withdrawal or stimulus seeking.

For the newborn child, the world is unknown and potentially confusing. The baby's physiological systems are immature and require time to adapt and stabilise. A newborn cannot immediately fit into routines and, as we have seen (Chapter 2), sensitive caregiving involves responding to the baby. If a baby is fortunate to receive 'responsive enough' care, the pattern that the brain slowly recognises is 'When I am uncomfortable, someone tries to help me'. This can be the very beginning of contingency recognition that can develop into competence.

In time, babies benefit from structure and routines which help provide a predictable pattern to their experience. The most important part of the consistent and predictable environment concerns interpersonal responses. Children whose carers reliably pay attention to, and interact, with them and who give largely consistent messages about boundaries, learn about their own effect on people. They learn that smiling generally invites very positive reactions. They learn how to make people laugh. They delight in their growing competence. A notable feature of developmental psychology research is increasing recognition that even very young babies initiate interaction and try to have an impact on their environment. Young children are very confused if normally interactive carers inhibit their usual responses. When a parent ceases normal interaction with a baby and instead keeps a straight, unresponsive face for a couple of minutes, the baby will try to secure a response from the parent by means such as smiling, pointing and making noises. If the parent remains unresponsive, the infant turns away and stops smiling. This 'still-face effect' has been repeatedly shown in experiments

(Adamson and Frick 2003) and indicates that babies are quickly aware of behaviour that contravenes their expectations.

The importance for well-being of having an environment that is predictable and over which one has some control has been known for some time. Classic animal experiments highlighting the importance of control were carried out by Seligman and colleagues in the 1960s (Overmeier and Seligman 1967; Seligman and Maier 1967). Ethical considerations would prevent such experiments nowadays. In brief, the experiments involved comparison of two groups of dogs (A and B) subjected to electric shocks. Each dog in group A was matched to one in group B. In part one of the experiment, the shocks occurred randomly but group A dogs could end the shock by pressing a lever. The matched dog in group B received shocks at the same time and for the same duration as the group A dog but it was only the group A dog that had control (by lever pressing) over the length of shock. In part two, all the dogs were given shocks but it was now possible for all to escape the shocks by jumping away. Group A jumped to avoid the shocks but group B did not. Their experience of lack of control in part one resulted in them failing to exercise control in part two – they had learned to be helpless (incompetent). Lack of control – rather than just exposure to electric shock – seemed to be the vital factor associated with animals becoming withdrawn and unable to cope. Possible parallels with abused children are disturbing.

In babies as young as 12 months, there is some experimental evidence that control may diminish fear of a potentially frightening object. Gunnar (1978, 1980) compared 1-year-old babies' reactions to a walking robot toy that was potentially frightening. Some children were able to control the toy's movement and noise by hitting a panel to activate it; other children could not. The children with control seemed less frightened by the toy and approached and touched it more often.

In toddlerhood, children begin to learn and understand that people can have different feelings and responses to the same thing. Securely attached toddlers have the security to explore how far they can challenge their caregivers' restrictions and the reactions they can evoke. Children from chaotic homes lack the predictable backdrop to their days and there are fewer patterns for them to detect, often resulting in less security. If carers are erratic, sometimes bestowing attention and at other times distant and unresponsive (as associated with ambivalent attachment, see Chapter 3), children's own actions are less predictable in their effects. A smile that may engage attention on some occasions can meet with disinterest or irritation on others. The link between cause and effect is unclear and so anxiety rather than competence is engendered.

Just as we discussed 'good enough' parenting, so too should we think in terms of 'good enough' predictability of routines and reactions in fostering children's competency. Rigid routines can be controlling and complete standardisation of reactions would be unnatural. Both would be unhelpful for a child's development. The brain is a good enough pattern detector to recognise broad patterns within minor everyday variations. The minor everyday variations may in fact help foster resilience (Chorpita and Barlow 1998). Children grow into their culture and much of what many parents and carers instinctively provide for children is appropriate for developing their competence and promoting positive behaviour.

There are, however, some children who are much more dependent than most on fixed routines. Whereas most children thrive on some novelty and variety, a few children become exceedingly anxious about even very slight changes. Such children benefit from warnings of the transitions within the usual day (for example, a bell five minutes before children have to come in from the garden, a five-minute sand timer counting down the final five minutes of a favourite activity). More major changes, such as an outing, need careful preparation. Some practitioners find an 'Oops card' on the visual timetable can be useful to alert a child to last-minute changes, such as a change in the plan to use the outside area if workmen arrive to fix the fence.

The importance of intrinsic motivation

Reflection 7.1

- What do you enjoy doing? If you were given a day free from duties and mundane tasks, how would you spend it?
- How often do you get the chance to do activities purely for enjoyment, activities that are intrinsically motivating for you?

Intrinsically motivating activities are those that people choose to do for their own pleasure. For adults, these are often hobbies, though fortunate adults find parts of their paid employment intrinsically motivating. People may put a great deal of effort into intrinsically motivating activities and can become engrossed, whether it is researching a family tree, tending an allotment or playing with their children. **Intrinsic motivation** is associated with engagement, deep learning, persistence, creativity and feelings of well-being. Csikszentmihalyi (1975) coined the term 'flow' to capture how outside concerns drop away and involvement in the activity becomes everything when one is deeply engrossed in intrinsically rewarding activities. There is an overlap between the ideas of intrinsic motivation and recreation (literally re-creation, being created again), with the latter term capturing the replenishing effects of following one's own interests. Recreation has been crowded out of some adults' lives, probably with detrimental effects to their health and well-being.

It is vital for children to have access to the opportunities for competence (and autonomy and learning) afforded by their intrinsic motivation. Young children do not have the '**executive functions**' (Chapter 9) required to fall in with someone else's agenda. Engaging in intrinsically motivating activities is the most effective way of developing feelings of competence and positive dispositions towards learning. It can also give a child a sense of well-being that might promote resilience and provide a buffer against the many challenges and setbacks that form part of life. Reference has been made earlier to Seligman's (2011) argument that well-being is about much more than the absence of negative outcomes; it requires also the presence of positive factors. Enjoying intrinsically motivating activities may be an important part of flourishing. When a child's behaviour is of concern to adults and there is a prolonged pattern of the child behaving in a way that suggests the basic psychological needs are not being met, any programme put in place to help the child should include opportunities for intrinsically rewarding activities. It is important to build up areas of potential strength and resilience as well as (or rather as part of) addressing behaviours of concern.

Case snippet 7.1: Jordan

Jordan is a quiet child who rarely says anything and who seems to become anxious when addressed directly. Helen, his Key Person, is increasingly concerned that he seems not just shy but withdrawn. She finds it difficult to gauge his language levels because he talks so little, either with adults or other children. She worries that his lack of verbal interaction is slowing his development. A different side to Jordan is seen when music plays. Jordan loves to dance! He loses his self-consciousness and moves to the music. Realising this, Helen plays music more often. She starts to dance too, at first some distance away from Jordan but, over a series of occasions, getting closer to him and finally catching his eye and clearly imitating his movements. A connection is made in this way and Jordan begins to look for Helen when the music comes on and he starts to dance. The dances become a form of turn-taking and communication. Now Jordan will pick up and copy some of Helen's moves in addition to smiling when she copies his. Over time, Jordan is increasingly confident across contexts. Helen's sensitivity to his intrinsic enjoyment of dance provided a key to unlocking more interactive behaviour.

The EYFS (DfE 2014b) acknowledges the importance of recognising and building on children's interests. This relates to harnessing intrinsic motivation. The early years curriculum is not about delivering set content but about fostering the effective characteristics of learning through activities that reflect or stimulate the children's interest. There is a developmental pattern to the types of activity that children tend to find interesting and intrinsically motivating. The Vygotskian tradition uses the concept of '**leading activities**' (Bodrova and Leong 2007). Leading activities are defined as the activities which are most beneficial for a child at a given stage of development and which have the most impact on subsequent development. Barring adverse experiences or additional needs, children tend to be intrinsically motivated by the leading activity for their developmental stage. Emotional interaction is held to be the leading activity for babies; exploring and playing with objects is the leading activity for toddlers; and imaginative play holds this status for pre-schoolers. Not surprisingly from an evolutionary perspective, there appear to be links between what children are intrinsically motivated to do, the activities that will help them develop competence and the activities that are most beneficial for their development (the 'leading activities'). By and large, one can work with children's natural drives rather than struggling to impose developmentally less appropriate styles of learning.

The depiction of emotional interactions with caregivers as the leading activity of infancy is consonant with the exploration of attachment theory in Part 1 and with the discussion above about how contingencies in social interaction contribute to feelings of competence.

Toddlers love cause-and-effect toys and benefit from the opportunities to explore a range of objects. The 'heuristic play' approach (Goldschmied and Jackson 2004) stresses that everyday objects made from a range of natural materials provide richer learning experiences than do plastic toys. Treasure baskets (Goldschmied and Jackson 2004) represent one way of ensuring that children benefit from a variety of textures and other sensory properties in their play. Exploring how objects work and what they can make objects do, is one of the ways toddlers develop feelings of competence in the physical world. A parallel strand of learning about social competence comes from others' reactions to their behaviour – what they are allowed to do and what adults prefer them not to do and how far they can go in 'testing' the adult's prohibition. Children are primed to learn and to revel in stretching themselves. They need opportunities to be out and about, exploring the physical world and opportunities for sustained interaction with others. Challenge plays a sometimes overlooked role in well-being. Adults may concentrate so much on trying to change the behaviour of a child who causes concern that they lose sight of the child's overall needs. Stimulus, excitement and challenge should be available to all children.

Imaginary play – the leading activity in the pre-school period – is considered by many psychologists and educators to be a hugely important vehicle for learning, developing among other things, symbolic understanding (Leslie 1987), understanding of rules (Vygotsky [1930] 1978), perspective taking (Evangelou et al. 2009: 22), flexibility of thought, social skills including co-operation (Goswami and Bryant 2007: 12), emotional understanding and self-regulation (Galyer and Evans 2001; Savina 2014). The pre-schooler who engages in intense imaginative play is also laying down sound foundations for the development of literacy (Bergen and Mauer 2000). Imaginative play is thus a prime context for the development of competence in a host of spheres, many of them with links to behaviour. This will be further explored in Chapter 9. For most children, and this includes children of school age, play is an intrinsically motivating activity. When trying to give a child the maximal opportunities to engage in activities that are intrinsically rewarding – part of any behaviour plan for a child causing concern – play may often be an activity to facilitate.

What about children who show limited intrinsic motivation? Occasionally children may show little motivation to do anything; they may appear listless and apathetic. This merits some investigation. It is important to establish the developmental history of such children, to check that they have not been traumatised and that they have received sufficient stimulation. Practitioners may have to be inventive in finding ways of stimulating and extending the child's interest. It is likely that other professionals should be involved to make suggestions and monitor the child's development.

Other children may show strong intrinsic motivation but only for a restricted range of activities. Here the challenge is to try to interest the child in a wider range of activities, sometimes by using the preferred activity as a 'way in'. A child who loves the train set might be enticed to wider interests if a train is taken with him to 'observe' or if the activity involves making a junk model structure for the trains. Sometimes a child's limited and intense interest will be unusual, for example, tapping on parts of the wall or removing the top of toilet cisterns to play with the ballcock. If normal, mild discouragement (with reasons given) to desist from such an activity is ineffective, it may be wise to consider to what extent arrangements can be made to permit the activity safely. Tapping on the wall may not be really problematic; playing with ballcocks is much more likely to be. Even in this case, it may be possible to capture some of the interest through water play involving a clean ballcock and opportunity to try to make it work as a valve. Children with restricted interests should be monitored carefully and other professionals involved if efforts to extend their interests meet with limited success.

Intrinsic motivation: treat with care!

Intrinsic motivation can be accidentally damaged by providing contingent rewards. We usually think that when we reward someone for something, we are encouraging them to repeat the behaviour or activity concerned. This is the central tenet of behaviourism. The surprising experimental finding that contingent reward could undermine motivation for intrinsically motivated activities highlighted the shortcomings of existing motivation theories and was a significant stimulus for Deci and Ryan's (2000) formulation of self-determination theory. In one study, Lepper et al. (1973) noted children in a pre-school setting who loved to draw. Later, some of these children (the experimental group) were given a **contingent reward** for their drawing ('If you draw, then you'll get ...'). Other children (control group 1) were given a non-contingent reward (a reward given unexpectedly after they had engaged in some drawing) and yet others (control group 2) received no rewards. Subsequent observations indicated that the children who had received contingent rewards chose drawing as a preferred activity after the experiment less often than they had before, whereas no such decline in drawing activity was found for the children in the control groups. Contingent reward for an intrinsically motivated activity reduces the frequency with which children engage in it.

Deci and Ryan later made sense of this finding in terms of how contingent rewards affect feelings of autonomy (psychological control) which, as we have seen, feature centre-stage in self-determination theory. Contingent reward for an intrinsically rewarding activity can dent that intrinsic motivation by making people feel more externally controlled.

Box 7.1: Theory into practice

To help promote intrinsic motivation, you should:

- Provide a wide range of stimulating opportunities for children.
- When children are deeply involved in an activity, try not to take them away from it unnecessarily.
- Notice children's interests and try to provide some extra challenge. Put some additional materials nearby. Allow children to bring materials from other areas of the setting. Ask open-ended questions such as 'What do you think would happen if ....?' (but back off if adult intervention seems to detract from their involvement and enjoyment).
- Talk about what they are doing, what they enjoyed, what went well and what did not, and their ideas about doing it again. Show genuine interest.
- Be careful with your use of praise and rewards. By definition, intrinsically motivating activities do not require external validation.

A 'growth mindset'

Reflection 7.2

Think about the last time you received praise. What were you praised for? When was the last time you praised someone and what did you praise? How important do you think praise is for yourself and for children?

The use of positive language with children is accepted normal practice in care and education settings. Practitioners are generally aware that the 'right' way to promote positive behaviour is to reinforce/praise good behaviour in preference to punishing unwanted behaviour. Practitioners can model and recommend a positive approach to parents or carers who may seem critical of children, for example, they 'catch them being good'. This technique involves withholding attention from minor incidents of unwanted behaviour and switching attention and taking care to make positive comments when the child behaves well. It is very important for there to be warmth in the relationships between children and those caring for them and the balance of positive to negative comments directed at a child can be one measure of this. Indeed, children from lower socio-economic classes tend, on average, to receive more parental criticism and less praise than those from higher socio-economic classes (Hart and Risley 1995) and a common and crucial thread of programmes aiming to help is to encourage parents and children to enjoy each other's company more. Increased use of praise can be both a technique to promote happier interaction and a sign that it is taking place. So important is this considered that Leicester runs a 'five a day' programme, echoing the well-known public health campaign to eat five servings of fruit and vegetables a day, encouraging parents to praise their children at least five times a day (Sutton 2012).

Praise has a role but an increasing body of research encourages us to consider whether we are balanced and discriminating enough in the praise we offer children. From the 1970s onwards the self-esteem movement was powerful, influencing many parents and practitioners alike (Noble and McGrath 2013). With its roots in Carl Rogers' idea (1961: 283) that children need unconditional positive regard (to be loved irrespective of what they do), the self-esteem movement banished criticism and ladled praise indiscriminately on children. The view was that children need high self-esteem in order to thrive. Low self-esteem was seen as the root of many problems, from fear of 'having a go' at new experiences, be they social encounters or learning challenges, to lacking confidence in one's own judgement and being unduly influenced by peers. Low self-esteem was regarded as a contributory cause of underachievement and behavioural issues. Praise was thought to foster high self-esteem which in turn would promote achievement on all fronts. Exceedingly limited evidence has been found for the supposed benefits of high self-esteem (Baumeister et al. 2003) and there have been extensive critiques of a bland, pervasive praise strategy. This has led to a more nuanced understanding of praise and its effects.

Stanford psychologist Carol Dweck has been particularly interested in the mental representations children form of their competency and autonomy and how these impact over time on their well-being and behaviour. She coined the term '**mindset**' to capture differing patterns of beliefs or mental representations (**internalisations**) that people form. She argues that people tend to view the world through either a 'fixed' or a 'growth' mindset (Dweck 2008) and has developed questionnaires that can reliably identify the nature of an individual's mindset. Those with a growth mindset feel that what they do makes a difference: it is worthwhile for them to strive to achieve the behavioural and other standards they set for themselves; none of their abilities is set, they can all be developed further with effort (Table 7.1). They are self-motivated, purposeful people who are not only willing to face challenges but positively embrace them. In a vast body of experimental work (for example, Diener and Dweck 1978; Mueller and Dweck 1998), Dweck has demonstrated that failure undermines performance for people with a fixed mindset but enhances it for those with a growth mindset. She has also shown how interventions (such as teaching about the brain as a muscle that can grow with exercise, or telling inspirational stories of the striving behind individuals' achievements) can influence people towards a growth mindset. A growth mindset is a vital component of competence. It also links clearly with the characteristics of effective learning in the EYFS.

Table 7.1 Beliefs and behaviours associated with fixed and growth mindsets

Fixed mindset	Growth mindset
I am at a fixed point on the good/bad, clever/not clever and other similar scales. That's how I am. I can do nothing to move up the scale.	I can develop (grow) any and all of my capacities through effort.
I must put on as good a 'front' as possible. My true self is not good enough and I need to hide my shortcomings so that I don't lose the love and positive regard people have for me.	What matters is making progress and enjoying the stimulus of learning or managing to achieve something new. It's intrinsically motivating.
If things go badly, there's nothing I can do. I might as well give up. It's better not to attempt things that might go wrong – that way I avoid showing myself up.	The more challenging I find something, the more effort I put in and the better it is when I finally get to grips with it.

Source: Based on Dweck (2008).

Much of this book is about approaches that support children's development in ways that meet their emotional needs and enable them to delight in their interactions and learning. Many of the approaches already discussed will contribute to the development of a growth mindset in children. Dweck's work, however, shines a spotlight on the use of praise. She argues that **'person praise'** focusing on a person's qualities ('you're a good girl', 'you're a clever boy') or their achievements ('Wow! You built that gigantic tower!') does not boost their competence as intended. Instead, over time, it has a detrimental effect. Children praised mainly for their cleverness or conforming behaviour are at risk of developing an internal representation that sees their worth as dependent on continuing to excel in these spheres. The prospect of performing less than perfectly becomes scary as it might result in being loved or liked less. Children start to avoid challenges, through fear of failure, and they try to cover up achievements or behaviour that might earn condemnation.

There are some indications that girls from at least middle childhood may be more susceptible than boys to the unintended detrimental effects of 'person praise' (Corpus and Lepper 2007). Dweck (2000) argues that bright girls are particularly vulnerable to the factors that foster fixed mindsets and to internalised behaviour difficulties in the longer term as a result of not feeling competent or autonomous, despite often behaving 'well' and achieving at high levels. The high level of 'person praise' they have achieved is regarded as contributing to the problem.

The type of praise or feedback that Dweck advocates is **process praise** which comments on effort, perseverance and strategies (see Box 7.2).

Box 7.2: Process praise

- 'You told Monika that it upsets you when she takes things without asking – it's good to tell her that so that she knows.'
- 'Taking turns – that was a good way for you both to be able to play.'
- 'You asked Elliot if you could go next – that was a good way to get the bike.'
- 'Ah, you're matching the colours – that should work well.'
- 'You're looking carefully at the shapes – good.'
- 'Pouring the water like that didn't work? You're trying another way now. Good idea!'
- 'You shared the banana pieces very carefully.'
- 'You made a really tall tower using the big bricks at the bottom.'

Most of Dweck's work has consisted of experiments. Only recently have she and her colleagues published longitudinal naturalistic observational research which investigates whether naturally occurring praise relates to mindsets in the way their ideas would predict. Gunderson et al. (2013), under the guise of studying language development, took videos of parent–child interactions when children were aged 14, 26 and 38 months. These were analysed for the amount and nature of spontaneously occurring praise. Later, when they were 7–8 years old, children's mindsets were ascertained using questionnaires. The findings indicated that frequency of process praise correlated with a growth mindset, suggesting that this type of praise may be particularly influential in fostering competence. It was noted that while parents did not differ in rates of praise for sons and daughters, more of that praise tended to be process praise in the case of sons. This has also been found to be true of teachers (Dweck et al. 1978).

With the young children in the Gunderson et al. (2013) study, 'person praise' did not in fact correlate with fixed mindsets, though the researchers had hypothesised that it might. Parents used significantly less 'person praise' with their 38-month-old children than when they were younger. The authors speculate that phrases they counted as 'person praise' (such as 'good boy') may be quite different in terms on effects on different ages of children. Praise and feedback have to be appropriate for children's language comprehension and it may be that 'good boy' and similar short expressions carry just a positive message for very young children. It is possible that, as children's language comprehension develops, 'person praise' may affect their mental representations towards a fixed mindset over time. As soon as their language comprehension allows, it may be particularly important when correcting children's unacceptable behaviour to give them 'process' messages about the behaviour required rather than the 'person message' that the child is 'bad'. Children form ideas of goodness and badness from a very early age (Dweck 2000: 96) and a fixed view of the self as 'bad' could impede the development of positive behaviour.

Reflection 7.3

- Do you think you have a fixed or a growth mindset?
- What sort of praise and feedback did you receive when you were growing up?
- Did you feel you had to get things right first time, or was it more about doing your best and improving over time?
- Think about the areas of endeavour that were important in your family – sports activities, music, schoolwork, behaviour.
- If you had siblings of a different gender, think whether your parents gave different messages to boys and girls.

In addition to process praise and feedback, there are other approaches that seem likely to foster positive reaction to challenge. The models children observe are likely to be important, so modelling making mistakes and recovering from them is likely to be helpful. As noted earlier, Dweck's experimental interventions suggest various helpful techniques such as telling stories of people who persisted despite setbacks and teaching about the brain as a muscle that improves with exercise.

Box 7.3: Theory into practice

Process praise and gender
Consider the following questions to help you translate theory into practice:

- Do you agree that boys tend to receive more process praise than girls?
- Audit the setting where you work for types of praise given to boys and to girls. Are boys receiving more process praise?
- Can efforts be made to increase the process praise given to all, and especially to girls?
- Think how the issues concerning praise can be shared with parents. Would a group discussion on this topic be something they might engage with?
- Could you write a short leaflet summarising key messages?

Key points

- Predictable environments foster competence.
- Intrinsic motivation is important for well-being. All children should have ample opportunities for intrinsically motivating activities and this is particularly true for children whose behaviour is a cause for concern.
- Promote opportunities for children to find intrinsically motivating activities by providing a wide range of activities to stimulate and interest them and allowing extended periods of time on activities that fire their enthusiasm.
- Show a genuine interest in the process of what children do and ask open questions and make process-related comments on the activities, concentrating on strategies, effort and persistence.
- Correct behaviour, where necessary, by giving clear process information regarding the preferred behaviour. If there is criticism, focus on the behaviour rather than the child (avoid person criticism).
- Remember that intrinsic motivation can be easily dented. Use praise sparingly and in a process manner when children are enjoying what they are doing.
- Model making mistakes at times.
- Tell stories, share books and recommend films that show characters succeeding through perseverance.

Further reading

Dweck, C.S. (2008) *Mindset. The New Psychology of Success*, New York: Ballantine Books.
This book is written for a popular, and not just an academic, audience and presents Carol Dweck's research and ideas in an accessible manner.

Early Education supported by the Department for Education (2012) *Development Matters in the Early Years Foundation Stage (EYFS)*, London: Early Education.
Development Matters unpacks the characteristics of effective learning, usefully highlighting what adults can do and provide. Many of these ideas relate very closely to fostering intrinsic motivation and growth mindsets and practitioners may find it helpful to revisit the characteristics of effective learning, having read this chapter.

8

Communication skills and behaviour
'I need to understand and make myself understood'

Of all the types of competence that might impact on behaviour, communication skills arguably hold a position of particular importance. Communication is a vast topic. This chapter will be selective, highlighting some issues relevant to behaviour but not aiming to provide comprehensive coverage. Sources of further information are signposted at the end of the chapter in the further reading section.

Do communication difficulties impact on behaviour?

Children who, for whatever reason, do not develop abilities to express themselves and to understand spoken and other communication at levels typical for their age are at a significant disadvantage. If children lack communication skills, they have limited means of securing what they want. They are more likely to take direct action (for example, by grabbing) if they lack the verbal skills for negotiating.

Studies indicate a correlation between language skills and behaviour difficulties (Royer 2013; Tommerdahl 2013). Ripley and Yuill (2005) assessed the language abilities of 19 boys who had been excluded from school and found that 13 of them displayed language problems. Schoon et al. (2010) studied data from the Birth Cohort Study which assessed 6,941 people at age 5 and followed them up 29 years later. Those with poor understanding of language at 5 years old were more likely to have experienced behavioural or mental health difficulties by adulthood. These studies are correlational and, as discussed in Chapter 1, correlations do not necessarily mean that one of the correlated factors is the cause of the other. However, as will be discussed below, some of the adult behaviours that promote healthy **internalisation/ socialisation** depend heavily on communication and language, and this lends weight to the argument that developing these skills is likely to help promote positive behaviour.

Communication is more than verbal language

Communication involves sending and receiving messages. Communication is so heavily intertwined with most aspects of development and with daily living that it can be difficult to tease out its contribution to socialisation and behaviour. Sociocultural theories essentially acknowledge the importance of communication in the broadest sense, stressing that children participate in a culture and that the culture both facilitates and shapes their development. A culture communicates its values and expectations in myriad ways, both non-verbally (for example, by facial and other 'body language' reactions to behaviour) and verbally (for example, by praising or condemning certain acts). While some communication is intentional (such as a parent frowning explicitly at children to indicate they should take no more biscuits at Grandma's tea table), other is unintentional (such as the flicker of dismay that might cross a mother's face and be spotted by Grandma when she produces another cake for the children). The intentional and unintentional aspects of communication are often congruent, but perhaps not as frequently as we may like to think. People commonly give mixed messages, saying one thing while their non-verbal communication gives a conflicting message. In the example of the mother who wants to limit her children's sugar consumption and who frowned when her mother-in-law produced a cake, it is possible that the mother would nevertheless thank her mother-in-law for a delicious cake for the children. Mixed messages abound. Non-verbal aspects of communication are often more reliable than verbal aspects. Children are typically astute at gauging the emotional tone of messages, including unintentional ones. A small number of children, however, struggle to decipher emotional tone and messages given through body language and these difficulties impact on their behaviour. So-called **social (pragmatic) communication** differences will be discussed again towards the end of the chapter.

Communication begins at birth (or earlier)

Communication begins at birth and attachment (Part 1) develops largely through non-verbal communication though, of course, adults speak to babies at the same time as rocking them, cuddling them and smiling at them, and this is valuable long before babies can understand the actual words said. Communication skills and attachment have the same roots – both develop out of the interaction between a baby or young child and other people. Communication is about much more than words – its foundations are turn-taking and reciprocity, and these can be fostered from birth.

Reflection 8.1

- How do you help parents to understand the importance of communicating and interacting with their baby from birth?
- Do you often see adults with young children chatting on their mobile phones rather than interacting with children?
- What are the advantages and disadvantages of buggies where the child faces the adult and those where the child faces in the direction of travel? Are there implications for communication?

'Motherese'

People tend to speak to babies in a simplified, singsong fashion which is known as '**motherese**' or 'infant-directed speech'. Occasionally people disparage this but 'motherese' occurs across cultures and has been found to promote children's verbal development (Parish-Morris et al. 2013). In baby rooms that are promoting communication (and thus contributing to the longer-term likelihood of positive behaviour), one would expect to see practitioners conversing with babies in infant-directed speech. They should also imitate babies' babble as babies will often respond to this by a turn-taking game in which they increase the babble during their turns, again practising foundational skills for communication (Reddy 2008).

Supplementing verbal language with visual cues

In any group of young children, verbal comprehension levels will vary. This is true even when all the children experience English as the language at home and in a setting. Frequently, a group setting will include children for whom English is an additional language. Bear in mind also that young children often suffer from ear infections, colds and other conditions which may intermittently affect their hearing. Learning language in context, with visual cues to tune the learner into the meaning, is the natural way to learn. For all these reasons, settings should support children's language comprehension and memory with visual cues. These might include:

- Showing children what terminology means – take them to what you are talking about or, where feasible, bring the relevant objects to the children and demonstrate any instructions you wish them to follow.
- Providing a simple commentary of the steps a child is following when learning a new routine or behaviour.
- A visual timetable, using photographs.
- Story sacks and song boxes with props.
- Makaton signing (always to be used with accompanying speech).

Often children may not catch or understand all that the adult says but will do the expected thing because of visual cues (including copying other children). This is fine. If, however, you begin to think that a child may understand very little language and be relying entirely on other cues, you may want to investigate further. A hearing test may be useful. You will need to test verbal comprehension by taking away the visual and other cues (including the subtle cues such as looking at the toys you mention) and seeing if the child can understand verbal directions. Children may easily guess certain actions that you are likely to ask for with given toys (for example, 'feed the dolly' if a doll, plate and fork are present). Ask for some less predictable actions as well ('put the fork under the plate') to be sure you are assessing language comprehension. It may be appropriate for a Speech and Language therapist to become involved to carry out a detailed and specialist assessment.

Vygotsky and the importance of language for behaviour

In Vygotskian theory (Bodrova and Leong 2007), language is regarded as essential for children's intellectual development and as playing a crucial role in their ability to regulate their behaviour. Particular attention is paid to the phenomenon of children talking to themselves as they concentrate on working something out (variously termed **'private' or 'egocentric' speech**). Young children quite commonly talk to themselves (and older people may too, especially when they think they are alone). For Vygotskians, the appearance of this type of speech indicates that children are using language as a tool for thought and are in the process of internalising the messages received from the cultural environment. The messages referred to are messages about regulating emotions and behaviour as well as messages about practical problem-solving. Vygotsky comments: 'It is decisively important that speech not only facilitates the child's effective manipulation of objects but also controls the *child's own behaviour*' ([1930] 1978: 26, italics in original). Vygotskians thus interpret it as a positive sign when children talk to themselves as it represents children working with the messages communicated to them and communicating with themselves to try to manage their emotions, behave in culturally acceptable ways or solve problems. 'Private' speech indicates developing competence. Adults should encourage it by preparing the groundwork for it, for example, by engaging in clear and timely explanation of rules and expectations, including mental state talk. They should also value 'private' speech when it is observed, leaving children free to see what they can manage on their own and only providing help when it is sought.

'Elaborative' talk

While communication always takes place in a variety of forms, spoken language gains in importance as children develop. Particular types of conversation help children to internalise cultural messages in a healthy manner. Also, while family members may be very attuned to each other without depending on words, verbal language tends to become increasingly important for communication as children broaden their social contexts and meet others who are less tuned into the subtle communicative intentions in their behaviour that may be understood at home.

Evangelou et al. (2009) stress the role of '**elaborative**' as opposed to descriptive talk in promoting children's social, emotional and behavioural development. Elaborative talk helps children make sense of events and emotions, it helps them evaluate things that have happened and relate them to other experiences. The following approaches discussed in Part 2 would come under the umbrella term of elaborative talk:

- emotion coaching;
- mental state talk;
- inductive discipline.

These approaches both develop and rely on linguistic competence. A child who cannot understand at age-typical levels may miss many of the nuances of the messages about behaviour being conveyed in the classroom and elsewhere. Behavioural problems may arise both because the child has not understood the messages about others' perspectives and feelings and so is not making the link between behaviour and its impact on others and also because of frustration with difficulties in understanding and in expression.

Social (pragmatic) communication

Reflection 8.2

When the volume control is silenced on the television but one continues to watch, it is usually easy to pick up the emotional tone of what is going on, whether people are calm or agitated, happy or angry. Try to imagine what it would be like not to be able to read body language. What problems would it create?

Many of us can think of a few people we do not quite 'gel' with, though it is hard to say exactly why. Often it will be because we find their body language hard to read, or ambivalent or just not in synchrony with our own.

For some people, it is the norm rather than the exception to miss or be baffled by body language. They find the social world an unpredictable, confusing place where they do not feel competent. Some would prefer to avoid it completely.

In discussing attachment, stress was laid on the importance of the attuned responsiveness of adults. Babies were portrayed as socially communicative and quick to establish how they can have an effect on adults' behaviour through, for example, crying and smiling (Table 8.1). This is true for the vast majority of babies.

Table 8.1 The socially communicative baby

Age	Communication
2–5 days old	Already I'm aware of who is paying me the most attention. I'll look more at someone who is watching me than at someone whose focus is elsewhere.
2 months	I can tell the difference between when your remarks are directed to me and when you are talking to someone else.
2 months	**Protoconversations.** When I smile at you and coo, these are my first conversations. I've yet to say words but I'm communicating and I'm already grasping important elements of conversation.
7–15 months	I love to interact with you and I'll smile, make noises and use all sorts of strategies to engage you and keep your attention.
9–18 months	**Joint attention** becoming established. I look where you look or where you point because I expect to find something interesting. I'll point things out to you too because I like to share things that interest me.
18–24 months	Now I can take turns in conversation for an increasingly long time.

Note: Babies are born with a disposition to look at human faces and to interact. The baby's voice aims to capture what experimental psychologists deduce from babies' behaviour.

There are, of course, individual differences in how long and how intensely babies like to interact. Some are significantly less drawn to communication or are less competent at aspects of it than the vast majority. At the extreme, a few appear to struggle with interaction and taking turns to the extent that attuned, sensitive adults minimise the interactive demands they make on the baby to avoid overwhelming a child who seems to find direct interaction aversive. Whereas most babies are frequently communicating, 'Notice me, play with me, respond to me', a few babies communicate 'Feed me and meet my physical needs but otherwise leave me be'. In much less extreme instances, there are babies who enjoy interaction but do not 'read' body language or transmit their signals with the ease of most babies.

Social (pragmatic) communication is a term used to capture the many aspects required for successful conversation beyond the words involved. Social (pragmatic) aspects include taking turns, acknowledging the partner's contribution, signalling a change of topic and adapting communication to take account of the partner's status (for example, talking differently to a teacher and a peer).

Children whose social (pragmatic) communication skills are not at levels typical for their age can inadvertently behave in ways that are considered rude or inept and this can get them into trouble.

Case snippet 8.1: Dominic

Miss Jones, the Reception teacher, is normally calm and approachable but one afternoon is very abrupt, firing out directions in a serious tone of voice. Most children pick up immediately that this she 'means business' at this moment and it would be best to fall in with her demands and save any requests or extraneous comments until a better time. Dominic does not read the cues. He is much slower than the others in coming to the carpet and when he sits down, he looks up and says, 'Oh, Miss Jones, are we going to the park for a Teddy Bear's Picnic next summer? My brother did when he was in your class'.

Luckily Miss Jones has realised that Dominic does not easily read social (pragmatic) communication cues and so she simply says: 'Dominic, you have to listen now. Mrs Burgess (teaching assistant) will talk to you in a moment.'

Adults need to be alert to the possibility that some children's 'poor' behaviour may result from difficulties with social (pragmatic) aspects of communication. Often adults are irritated by behaviour that violates pragmatic rules. Sometimes matters escalate, the adult becoming increasingly exasperated with a child who does not modify behaviour in the expected fashion. Many children, when under stress, find that their body language lets them down. They can grin with the embarrassment or tension of being under an adult's scrutiny for wrongdoing, a reaction that tends to make their situation worse. For children with problems in social (pragmatic) communication, giving out inappropriate signals is another manifestation of their (often misunderstood) problem. For children who do not pick up social communication cues and whose own body language does not 'help their cause', the social world can be an unpredictable and confusing place.

These children benefit from intentions and requirements being made much more explicit than usual. The adult may need to state, for example, 'Dominic, I'm not in the mood for people taking a long time to come to the carpet or asking me questions about the summer at the moment. I will be short-tempered if you don't do what I ask immediately like everyone else'. Adults need to coach children through situations in a clear, explicit way, for example, 'When someone is angry with you, and you are sorry, say "Sorry" and look down, keeping your mouth straight'. Sometimes it is appropriate to involve peers in coaching – 'If Ben comes too close to you when talking, say "Ben, you're too close. Step back a bit"'. Social stories (see Box 8.1) may also be helpful.

When children are learning skills from the specific areas of the EYFS, such as phonics or number bonds, we take it for granted that they need to learn a little at a time and to practise regularly to properly establish fluency in the skills. In the areas of social development and communication development, many children seem to absorb the skills so naturally that it can be overlooked that there are some children who require carefully structured programmes to build these skills systematically and to practise them so much that they become dispositions.

Box 8.1: Social stories

Social stories were devised and shared by Carol Gray (2001). They are a positive, clear way of alerting children to behavioural expectations. They should be personalised for a child, taking account of that child's concerns. Ideally they should be presented in a book and illustrated.

Here is a snippet from a story for a child who tends to shout when conversing and to stand so close to others that they find it uncomfortable:

> Miss Lewis will tell us when we have to be quiet and display the 'quiet working' sign. The rest of the time it is fine to talk to other people. I like to talk to people. It's good to share ideas and ask opinions. When I talk to people, I need to be one big step away from them. Most people like their 'personal space'. This is like an invisible bubble around them. If I go closer than one big step, people feel I am in their personal space and it makes them uncomfortable. I will stand one big step away from people. They might remind me if I forget and that is OK, I should just thank them, step back and carry on. I like talking to people and get excited when talking and want them to hear me. They can still hear me when I talk quietly. If I talk loudly, it can hurt their ears. I will talk quietly and it will be comfortable for them. We will have a good conversation.

Smith (2003) provides useful advice on social stories.

Key points

- Communication influences all aspects of development. Sociocultural theories encapsulate this.
- Communication in the broadest sense (non-intentional as well as intentional, non-verbal as well as verbal) is at the heart of socialisation and a vital aspect to consider with respect to behaviour.
- Speech and language skills play an increasing role in socialisation as young children develop. However, in optimum environments, these skills are being nurtured from birth.

COMMUNICATION SKILLS AND BEHAVIOUR 111

- 'Motherese' is helpful for babies and to be encouraged.
- An environment that promotes positive behaviour will take steps to communicate effectively and provide children with meaningful and varied opportunities to communicate.
- Visual 'props' (including visual timetables and gesture systems such as Makaton) can be useful for promoting understanding and predictability.
- 'Private' speech is to be valued and promoted as it can be seen as a step towards healthy internalisation of behaviour.
- Elaborative styles of adult–child interaction are associated with promoting positive behaviour.
- When behaviour of particular children is of concern, it is recommended to look in detail at their communication skills and to consider if support can be offered to develop them.
- Children with specific speech, language and communication needs are likely to require carefully structured programmes with frequent opportunities to practise and fully establish new skills as dispositions.

Further reading

Early Education supported by the Department for Education (2012) *Development Matters in the Early Years Foundation Stage (EYFS)*, London: Early Education.
Practitioners might find it useful to look at the section of *Development Matters* on 'Personal, Social and Emotional Development: Making Relationships'. A quick glance at the behaviours listed for babies highlights how interactive and communicative they tend to be from the very beginning. The detailed sections in *Development Matters* on 'Communication and Language' are valuable for reminding practitioners of the range of communication skills that typically develop and ways to promote them.

Every Child a Talker (ECAT). ECAT was a communication programme promoted by the government (DCSF 2008). Unfortunately it has now been archived although many practitioners continue to find it useful. Some information can be accessed at: http://webarchive.nationalarchives.gov.uk/20130401151715/https:/www.education.gov.uk/publications/eOrderingDownload/DCSF-00854-2008.pdf (accessed 30 October 2014).

EYFS Inclusion Development Programme, Speech, Language and Communication Needs. This was also a government-backed initiative, now archived. There is an e-learning course, open to all. Available at: http://webarchive.nationalarchives.gov.uk/20110202093118/http://nationalstrategies.standards.dcsf.gov.uk/node/174435 (accessed 30 October 2014).

ICAN, the children's communication charity, available at: www.ican.org.uk/en.aspx. A useful source of information, ideas and resources for supporting communication development.

9

Competence and executive functions

'I need the right sort of opportunities and support to practise skills such as paying attention, waiting and managing impulses'

Introduction

Emotions are our hot responses, valuable in many ways, as outlined in Chapter 5. Having only these 'hot' responses would be very limiting (and indeed 'emotion coaching', discussed in Chapter 5, takes children beyond the 'hot' response). Our ability to function well in the world depends on being able to moderate our 'hot' responses appropriately, being able to manage our impulses, to wait and reassess, to deliberately attend to certain things by choice, while blocking out distractions. If our emotions are like a thoroughbred horse – hot-blooded, sensitive, fast, 'highly strung'– we need to harness these qualities by developing the skills of a capable jockey. The horse on its own can run fast but is likely to veer off track and to be 'spooked' by noises and distractions around it. The jockey takes the reins and together horse and jockey may achieve great success.

Psychologists refer to the jockey skills as '**executive functions**'. Executive functions are essential if people are to have some choice and control over their behaviour, rather than being purely reactive. They are essential for effortful learning and for goal-directed activity. Hot emotional systems without jockey skills are bundles of energy, emitting emotions and emotionally driven behaviour all the time, flitting from one thing to another, grabbing what they want, pushing others out of the way or possibly attacking them if they put up resistance. (Readers may feel they recognise children in this category.) Jockey skills without a hot system are (well-programmed) computers, rather than people. They are rational but not human, lacking the intuition, the individual 'gut reactions' and drive that characterise people.

Executive functions describe an important set of skills that emerge during development and which are crucial for purposeful activity. Executive functions include being able to stop or delay responses; being able to direct attention; being able to formulate and hold in mind a plan; and being able to try alternative approaches if what you are doing is not working or the requirements of a task change. These skills are important for all of us to function effectively. Children whose executive function skills are poorly developed for their age will fall below age norms for behaviour and learning. Pre-schoolers considered as exhibiting problem behaviours show poor executive functioning for their age (Hughes and Dunn 2000). Research suggests that executive functioning plays a significant part in school readiness (Bierman et al. 2008; Welsh et al. 2010).

The terminology used by different researchers varies but executive functions can be considered in three main groupings (Diamond 2013):

1   *Working memory* – being able to hold and manipulate ideas in memory, making connections with previous events and ideas.
2   *Inhibition* – inhibiting (holding back) impulses, being able to wait. Keeping unwanted/distracting thoughts at bay.
3   *Cognitive flexibility* – not being 'stuck' on one way of doing or thinking about things but being able to switch strategies or entertain alternative interpretations.

Executive functions underpin both socio-emotional and intellectual problem solving. In this chapter the emphasis is more on the socio-emotional aspect and its links with behaviour.

Working memory

Working memory refers to the capacity to both hold and manipulate items in short-term memory. Working memory is not just passive retention of material, it is active engagement with the material, making connections with previous experience and knowledge. If someone says the names of three things to you and asks you to repeat them back, that is a short-term memory task. If, however, they name three things and you have to say them back in the order 'most like to least like', it becomes a working memory task because you are required to work out the order. Working memory is an important component of many aspects of behaviour and learning. Deciding on and executing any sort of plan requires working memory. Mulling over events or things that have been said involves working memory if, as is usually the case, you are not just recalling but trying to make sense of what has happened and planning whether and how to respond. Working memory is involved in relating things that happened earlier to things that have just happened, noting similarities and puzzling over differences. It is part of the reflection that informs social understanding and helps us formulate responses.

Inhibition

Walter Mischel is a professor at Columbia University, New York. When he worked at Stanford University in California in the late 1960s he started his now famous marshmallow experiments on delayed gratification at the Bing nursery, the childcare facility provided for those working at the university and attended by his young daughters. Mischel perfected the form of his marshmallow experiment by trying out various forms with his daughters around their kitchen table.

In the classic form of the experiment, young children who have indicated that they like marshmallows are seated at a table in front of a marshmallow and offered a choice: have one marshmallow now or wait until the adult comes back and, if they have not eaten the single marshmallow, they can have two. Children have a bell to summon the adult if they decide they cannot wait. The experiment is about delayed gratification. Can children wait for something they want, if waiting increases the amount they get? The results were measurements of the number of seconds' delay the children waited.

What were the important findings?

- Not surprisingly, children's ability to wait for the two marshmallows (to delay gratification) improved with age.
- As they grow, children develop their ideas about helpful strategies:
  - Children aged $3^1/_2$ –4-years-old thought it would help them to look at the marshmallows.
  - 4- and 5-year-olds often realised that covering the marshmallows or looking away from them would make the wait easier.
  - Some 4-year-olds and many 5-year-olds spontaneously used strategies such as repeating the contingencies to themselves ('If I wait until she comes back, I'll get two') or distracting themselves by jiggling their legs or twiddling with their hair.

Mischel and his team carried out some versions where children were encouraged to think about the marshmallows in particular ways while waiting:

- Some were encouraged to think about the lovely sweet taste and melting softness in the mouth they would have when they ate the marshmallow.
- Others were encouraged to think about the marshmallows in terms of aspects other than their taste and factors associated with eating them. They might, for example, think of the marshmallows as soft pillows or beanbag chairs for toy figures or as little clouds.

COMPETENCE AND EXECUTIVE FUNCTIONS 115

You can probably guess the results!

- Thinking about the taste reduced the ability to delay.
- Thinking about the marshmallows as something other than food significantly increased ability to delay.

Mischel's daughters were close in age to the first cohort of young children who took part in the marshmallow experiments. Ten years or so later, when the girls were adolescents and chatting about friends and their varied escapades, Mischel had a 'light bulb moment'. He realised that it would be fascinating to follow up the young children who had taken part in the marshmallow experiments. He collected data from their high schools and he and his research team continue to track some of original cohort now, more than 40 years on. All the data from this longitudinal research show that differences in delay in gratification at age 4 correlate with significant outcomes over time. In high school the children who could delay gratification as youngsters were socially and emotionally well-adjusted and achieved well. Children with very short delay times at age 4 had significant problems with behaviour and were failing academically in adolescence. This pattern has continued in the subsequent follow-up studies. Ability to delay gratification at age 4 seems to have huge implications for a child's future behaviour, achievement and overall adjustment (Mischel et al. 1989; Hammond 2011).

One form of inhibition is the delayed gratification called for in the marshmallow experiment (see Box 9.1). Successful inhibition of many sorts is required if children are to be able to get on with others and to learn effectively. In many situations it is best to curb (inhibit) an immediate emotional response to a situation and give ourselves time to consider how to interpret it and how to react. In order to complete activities efficiently, we need to focus and limit our responses to distractions, for example, listening to a story requires maintenance of attention. Children who are learning about how to ask for something nicely rather than grab may know cognitively what they should do but will only be successful if they can manage to inhibit the impulse to grab.

Cognitive flexibility

Cognitive flexibility is the third building block of executive functions and the latest of the three to develop. It refers to the ability to vary your approach to things and entertain different perspectives. It is necessary when your usual or previous response becomes ineffective but it is also helpful much more broadly. It can enable people to find creative and better ways of doing things. In the realm of behaviour, cognitive flexibility is associated with being open-minded in judgements of people and recognising that situations can be interpreted and reacted to in a variety of ways. Inflexibility, on the other hand, is manifest when people are very rigid in their interpretations and reactions. Children who very quickly take offence and react aggressively to their peers often show lack of cognitive flexibility. An incident such as a child knocking against their toys, that looks accidental and that many children would be likely to ignore or respond to in a low-key fashion, can elicit a major and negative reaction from a child with very limited cognitive flexibility.

Mischel et al.'s (1989) findings of the relationship between delayed gratification in the early years and later adult adjustment and well-being have been noted in Box 9.1. There is other evidence about the long-term significance of executive functions, a particularly noteworthy study being that carried out by Moffitt and her colleagues in New Zealand (Moffitt et al. 2011). This longitudinal study followed children from birth to age 32 years and found that poor self-control in childhood predicted criminal offending, substance abuse, poor physical health, and financial problems. Conversely, the better a child's self-control, the better the long-term outcomes were likely to be. These studies highlight the importance of executive functions. Other sources of evidence indicate that children (and older people) can be helped to improve their executive functions, making this a fruitful area for building skills to make a difference in children's prospects. Adele Diamond is a leading researcher in the area of executive functions and makes strong arguments that building up children's executive functions holds out the potential for reducing the difference in outcomes between children from advantaged and disadvantaged backgrounds (Diamond and Lee 2011; Diamond 2013).

The development of executive functions

Executive functions are associated with the pre-frontal cortex, an area of the brain that shows particularly rapid development between 3 and 6 years of age. This is a key time for the development of executive functions but they continue to develop into adulthood. The three categories of executive function show different developmental timelines – working memory develops earliest, inhibition is the next to begin to appear and cognitive flexibility is the last.

What builds executive functions?

Recent work on executive functions derives from neuropsychology but Vygotsky's sociocultural ideas provide a theoretical framework that continues to be useful for thinking about the development of these functions and the adult role in facilitating this.

The crux of the Vygotskian view of development is that children interact with the people and materials surrounding them and that this interaction is not only necessary to stimulate development but influences the form of the development that takes place. It is a theory that recognises that development is neither 'nature' or 'nurture' alone but an interaction, such that the type of nurture influences which of the inbuilt potentials flourish and which fade. The executive functions developed by children will depend on their biological make-up but also, crucially, on the strategies modelled and encouraged by the people with whom they interact and wider cultural aspects.

Vygotskians refer to the development of **mental tools** (or **tools of the mind**) to describe and explain how children move from immediately reacting to stimuli to being able to plan, focus and persevere. Mental tools and executive functions can be seen as largely similar. In Vygotskian theory, the acquisition of mental tools is crucial for self regulation of both behaviour and learning, and comes about as a result of social interaction. It is through the process of interaction that children learn, for example, ways of focusing their attention, inhibiting their impulses and directing their behaviour and learning towards goals. The quality and nature of the social interactions available to children can help or hinder the acquisition of mental tools/executive functions.

Vygotsky believed that children first learn through active engagement (co-construction) with others and later internalise the strategies that can support their learning. In Part 1 there was reference to the idea that securely attached infants are calmed by their carers and through this learn, over time, to calm themselves. The idea here is similar. Mutual processes lay the foundations for independent processes. When adults create the conditions for children to engage in activities that interest and stimulate them, and when they or other children support the child in developing strategies for persistence and constructive problem solving, then the child will, over time, adopt such strategies independently. The facilitation role is not to do with the transmission of information. It is to do with providing the degree of challenge and support appropriate to individual children engaging in activities that are meaningful to them. The Vygotskian term, '**zone of proximal development**' (ZPD) is used to capture the area of learning where facilitation by more knowledgeable others is most effective. The ZPD is just above where a child can function independently but where success is still possible with sensitive support. It is through the process of interaction that children learn, for example, ways of focusing their attention, inhibiting their impulses and directing their behaviour and learning towards goals.

Vygotsky's contribution to the fields of psychology and education has been immense. He died in 1934, aged only 37. His ideas have been developed and applied by researchers from his native Russia and other countries and it is the work of these Vygotskians, particularly Bodrova and Leong (2007) that usefully links to executive functions and behaviour. Bodrova and Leong (2007) developed an approach known as 'tools of the mind' which has been enthusiastically adopted in many pre-schools in the United States and which has attracted attention for the high level of children's executive functioning (Diamond and Lee 2011) and their behaviour (Bronson and Merryman 2010).

The value of language as a mental tool was mentioned in Chapter 8 which highlighted private speech as a means of the child beginning to internalise behaviours. Private speech bridges or mediates between regulation by others and self-regulation.

Imaginary or make-believe play has particular importance in Vygotskian theory. In Chapter 7 its designation as the leading activity of pre-schoolers was noted. Imaginary play is seen as a prime context for the development of executive functions. Vygotsky stressed that play involves rules – in being a 'mummy' or a 'baby', children choose to follow what they regard as the rules of mummy or baby behaviour. The setting aside of children's own persona and the deliberate adopting of another both require and further develop executive functions. In imaginary play a prop can stand for something else or children can just pretend that, for example, they are driving a car. This symbolisation requires overriding of the here and now, with reference to a plan formed through imagination – again, features of executive functioning are apparent and become strengthened through this type of play (Savina 2014). Imaginary plays involves talk in the roles assumed and also talk outside these roles to negotiate the course of the narrative with others involved – it thus involves mental flexibility to keep track of the different rules required in role and as an out-of-role negotiator on behalf of one's role! The interaction among children in play is the medium through which they regulate each other and learn in time to regulate themselves. The richness of children's mental state talk in shared imaginary play has already been alluded to (Brown et al. 1996, Chapter 6). The tools of the mind curriculum emphasises sustained imaginary play for pre-schoolers. From an early age children are encouraged and supported to plan and review their play. These processes have been shown to lead to more mature and sustained play (Bodrova and Leong 2007), while the planning and reviewing are themselves processes that build executive functioning.

Reflection 9.1

- Which activities do you do with children that support the development of their executive functions?
- Consider the three main components of executive functioning in turn: working memory; inhibition; and cognitive flexibility.

Looking through an 'executive functions lens', it can be recognised that many traditional activities carried out with young children are likely to develop these skills (Tominey 2011). Games such as 'Simon Says', 'Musical Statues' and 'Grandma's Footsteps' require skills of motor inhibition. The card game of 'Pairs' where children have to remember the position of cards previously seen and turn over the correct one to match a given card, calls on working memory. The game where children have to identify photographs of objects taken from unusual angles requires one form of cognitive flexibility. Another type of flexibility is required to cope with changes of rules within games: at first, clap when you hear a word naming a food, then, after a few minutes, stop clapping for food and clap only for colours. Planning and reviewing by children are, as previously indicated, crucial activities for developing executive function.

Case snippet 9.1: Oliver

James, the Key Person, sits his key group in a quiet corner for a few minutes' conversation each day. Several of the children are always eager to talk. Oliver tends to dominate, being an articulate boy with much to say. James feels that the children would benefit if the conversations were less of a 'free for all'. He tells the children that he is going to introduce a thinking pause when he asks them something he wants them to think carefully about. During the thinking pause, he and they are going to place their index finger on their closed lips. 'We all need a little time to work out our best answer to a question. Oliver, for example, you always have answers. Often you give one answer very quickly, then you think of an even better one and say that too. Now we are all going to pause and think of our best answer before we tell everyone else.' James now always uses the thinking pause at group time and models it at other times when he is asked questions through the day. The children become used to it. After some reminders, Oliver develops the habit of using his finger to remind him to pause.

Recently the setting invited a policewoman visitor to talk to the children. She invited them to ask questions. While one child was talking, James saw that Oliver was about to butt in. Catching Oliver's eye, James started to move his finger towards his mouth. Oliver immediately raised his own finger and successfully waited until an appropriate point to ask his question.

Most of us notice how we struggle with demanding tasks when we are tired or below par. Diamond (2013) notes that executive functions are adversely impacted by factors such as lack of sleep, stress or insufficient exercise. When children show delays in executive functioning, she urges an overall view of their lifestyle before assuming that they have a specific problem with executive functioning. Addressing sleep patterns or exercise patterns might in turn result in improved executive functioning.

Diamond (2013) also reports the research finding that in many situations a child's impulsive response is wrong but, if forced to wait, the same child can often achieve the correct response. The challenge for adults is to find ways of helping children slow down their wild horses and exercise their jockey skills!

Diamond and Lee (2011) reviewed the literature concerning interventions to promote the development of executive functions in children. Interestingly the effective interventions are quite varied and include the following (not in rank order for effectiveness):

- aerobic exercise
- martial arts
- mindfulness
- yoga
- CogMed – particular computer programmes designed to develop working memory
- bilingualism
- the tools of the mind curriculum (Bodrova and Leong 2007) (see Box 9.2 for related ideas)
- the Montessori curriculum (see Box 9.3)
- Promoting Alternative Thinking Strategies (PATHS) (Greenberg et al. 1995) – a curriculum designed to develop children's emotional and social understanding through age-appropriate, fun activities and links to real-life situations.

Box 9.2: Theory into practice

Developing tools of the mind: some ways adults can support the development of executive functions
- Talk through procedures, events and happenings with children as this helps give a structure to their experience.
- Model 'private speech' (Chapter 8) when you demonstrate things for children and encourage them to use private speech themselves.
- If a young child says, 'No, no, no' but then carries out the action that s/he clearly has some awareness is wrong, interpret this as a sign that the child is on the journey towards internalising the behavioural requirements. Be positive, for example, 'That's right, Chris. We don't want to jump in the deep puddles before putting wellies on. Now you'll need to change into dry socks'.
- Encourage children to plan their play. At its simplest this starts with children making a choice of which activity they want to do. Later this develops into a drawn or written plan with children indicating what they want to do, what they will need for it, who else will be involved and how. To begin with, planning takes place immediately before the play. Later, planning may stretch ahead.
- Accustom children to reviewing their play and activities before they move on to something else. Again, gradually increase the challenge of the 'review', working towards a continuous cycle of review informing a new plan, and so on.
- Give young children roles – being as quiet as a mouse, as still as a soldier on sentry duty.

- Provide visual cues for roles, for example, children hold a picture of an ear when they are in pairs and it is their turn to listen, they have the picture of a mouth when it is their turn to talk.
- When learning particular skills, get children to pick out the best example of the skill in their own and other people's work or behaviour.
- Use external **mediators** to help children regulate their behaviour, for example, a carpet square to 'contain' a restless child for short periods of sitting on the carpet. Make sure to use external mediators in a manner where they are a tool to help the child along the way to internal control.

Source: Based on Bodrova and Leong (2007).

It is interesting that some of the interventions which improve executive functions clearly involve the controlled combination of physical and psychological skills. Conventional martial arts involve controlled and disciplined movement which both engenders and benefits from a calm and focused mind. Similarly, mindfulness approaches use controlled breathing to quieten the mind and help inhibit distracting thoughts and improve focus on the body in the present.

Some of the effective interventions are specific in their effects. Thus, the computer programs that improve working memory do not improve other aspects of executive functioning such as flexibility. It is therefore important to prioritise use of the broader approaches which foster the gamut of executive skills. All approaches are effective only when they keep on gradually increasing the executive function demands on children. Curricular approaches such as tools of the mind and the Montessori approach (see Box 9.3) embed the development of executive functions. This is more effective than 'bolt-on' approaches that try to develop the skills in isolation (Diamond and Lee 2011).

Box 9.3: Maria Montessori (1870–1952): medical doctor and renowned educationalist

One of the first female doctors in Italy, Maria Montessori worked with children with learning difficulties and developed methods for all children that continue to be practised in many nurseries.

Montessori believed a major part of the teacher's role lay in preparing the environment to allow children to follow their individual interests and learn from constructive activity. She advocated a peaceful, quiet, uncluttered environment. She developed 'didactic apparatus', carefully designed to enable children to spot and correct their own errors and so to maximise

(Continued)

what they could learn from independent exploration ('auto education'). Montessorian activities challenge children as they develop, for example, walking along a line then doing this while carrying a spoonful of water without spilling (Diamond and Lee 2011). Young children were viewed by Montessori as powerful, self-motivated learners. A teacher should observe but intervene only when necessary – 'she may always be ready to supply the necessary help, but may never be the obstacle between the child and his experience' (Montessori [1914] 2005: 87). Montessori fostered purposeful activity, often involving real-life activities, among children. She believed strongly in children being given long periods of uninterrupted time to become deeply involved in their activities. Hers was an individual approach with children working alone or choosing to work with one or two others. Her approaches let a child plan and assume control of learning. She promoted development of children's language and of their social and emotional understanding, creating an ethos in which prosocial behaviour was valued.

Diamond and Lee (2011) report research showing that children from Montessori schools surpassed children from other schools in their development of executive functions.

It is interesting to note a contrast between the tools of the mind and the Montessori approach. The former accords high priority to imaginary play for pre-schoolers whereas the latter (in the original form) sidelines this form of play as unhelpful. Nevertheless both approaches impact positively on executive functioning. Executive functions can be developed in many ways, some of which have not been fully researched yet, though there is growing interest in the possible role of music and singing (Winsler et al. 2011).

Box 9.4: Theory into practice

Consider the following questions to help you translate theory into practice:

- Using a pause. Is it part of your practice to slow the pace slightly, to have a 'thinking pause'?
- Do you help children with strategies for waiting? Do you ask them how they might cope in a waiting situation and steer them towards helpful strategies? They are desperate for turn on the bike. Is it better to make them stand watching a child who currently has a bike, waiting for a turn or to have some way of registering a place in a queue (e.g. putting their photo on a picture of a bike) and to then be called over by a staff member when it is time for their turn?

- Do you encourage children to look at things from a variety of perspectives, both physical and psychological? Do you facilitate discussion of different viewpoints?
- Do you give an appropriate balance between routine and surprise? Do you provide some warning of a break from routine for very young children or those who struggle with flexibility, e.g. advance verbal warning supported with visual cues which remain present?
- Do you talk through what is going to happen and what has happened?
- Are children given opportunities to plan and review their activities?
- Are all practitioners aware of children's level of executive functions and are they providing practice and challenge for each child at an appropriate level? Are opportunities for this seized whenever they arise throughout a session and not confined to a particular part of the session dedicated to executive functions?

Key points

- Going beyond reacting to immediate stimuli requires executive functions – the 'jockey skills' for successful negotiation of the racecourse of life.
- Self-regulated behaviour and deliberate learning depend on executive functions. They play an important role in school readiness and in life trajectories.
- The executive functions fall into three main groups: working memory; inhibition; and cognitive flexibility. They start to develop in the order listed. Development to mature levels takes a considerable time but there is a particularly rapid period of development from 3–6 years of age.
- Lack of sleep, stress and insufficient exercise impede the development of executive functions.
- Children's experiences can promote the development of executive functions.
- Vygotsky's theory of sociocultural development of mental tools fits comfortably with recent neuropsychological work on executive functions. The tools of the mind curriculum translates Vygotskian theory into practice and has been shown to be effective in helping children develop executive functioning and self-regulation of behaviour.
- A range of other approaches or experiences, from traditional martial arts, to mindfulness, to bilingualism, have been found to benefit executive functioning and it is likely that further effective approaches will be identified.

Further reading

Bodrova, E. and Leong, D.J. (2007) *Tools of the Mind: The Vygotskian Approach to Early Childhood Education*, 2nd edn, Upper Saddle River, NJ: Pearson Merrill/Prentice Hall.
This is an extremely useful book. Chapter 5 on mediators explains their purpose clearly, with many practical examples.

Bronson, P. and Merryman, A. (2010) *Nurture Shock*, Reading: Ebury Press.
Chapter 8 is relevant for executive functions. Other chapters of this interesting book are also relevant to the themes discussed.

Early Education supported by the Department for Education (2012) *Development Matters in the Early Years Foundation Stage (EYFS)*, London: Early Education.

Aspects of the development of executive functions occur at various points of *Development Matters*. Look for relevant advice in the sections, Characteristics of Effective Learning and also in Communication and Language and in Physical Development.

Part 4
Collaborating for positive behaviour
'Together we can'

Introduction to Part 4

The emphasis so far has been on children's needs for relatedness, autonomy and competence. In this final part we consider how we can take into account the same psychological needs of parents and practitioners. This is never more important than when trying to devise an effective positive behaviour plan for a child whose behaviour is causing extreme concern.

Chapter 10 considers parents and Chapter 11 considers practitioners. Both chapters contain a case study. In real life, 'case studies' are dynamic and all involve children, parents and practitioners. The approach advocated in this book is one of hypothesis testing and a collaborative process. It can be difficult to capture within a static description of a case study the interplay of the different elements and ideas as a situation unfolds and changes over time. In devising a behaviour programme, practitioners need to liaise with parents and include their views and ideas within the behaviour plan if it is to have maximum effectiveness. For this reason it is important to avoid the impression that practitioners simply inform the parents about the plan. Nevertheless, practitioners who are asking parents in to discuss a child's behaviour do need to prepare carefully for the meeting if the time is to be used to good effect. Box P4.1 shows a possible outline for such a meeting and Figure P4.1 shows a proforma that practitioners might use to gather their ideas in advance of the meeting.

Box P4.1: Meeting format

- Thank attendees for coming, particularly parents.
- Introductions.
- Purpose: to share information about (child's name)'s behaviour with a view to drawing on everyone's views to find things we might be able to do to help.

- Pleased to have (child's name), outline strengths. Put behaviour in context (e.g. 'quite rare but still concerning', 'a couple of times a week which, while concerning, means there are more days that are fine than not').
- Ask parents 'How are you feeling about (child's name) at nursery?' How is (child's name) at home? (If relevant: And why do you think there is a difference?')
- Outline the concerns, giving information from observations.
- Suggest initial hypothesis, appropriately worded.
- Invite comments.
- Revise or refine hypothesis in the light of the discussion.
- Suggest ideas about ways forward:
  - at whole group level;
  - changes in the physical environment;
  - changes in how adults react;
  - strategies to support the child (**mediators**?);
  - positive target for child.
- Ask for ways parents can help.
- Ask for additional suggestions or modifications to suggestions.
- Stress that you will be providing positive experiences for the child not contingent on behaviour (and be prepared to justify).
- Agree review arrangements.

Thank everyone for coming and indicate your availability to parents in the next few days once they have had a chance to reflect on the meeting. Would they appreciate a phone call?

Note that the proforma highlights some of the key messages that have been stressed about behaviour, such as the importance of building relationships and the value of intrinsically motivating experiences. The case studies in the following chapters use this proforma to capture the relevant information. Blank copies of the meeting format and the proforma are also included as Appendices 1 and 2 to allow ease of photocopying for readers' own use.

The case study in Chapter 10 involves a parent whose sense of competence seems to be threatened by hearing about her child's behaviour, a common scenario. In Chapter 11 a teacher struggles with the feelings engendered by the difficulty of forming a relationship with a child. The case studies try to capture some of the process of interpreting behaviour through the self-determination model (Deci and Ryan 2000), applying the model to the various 'players' and thinking about the underlying needs yet translating the insights into constructive action for those involved. Note when you read the case studies that the targets proposed for children are not in terms of things they should stop doing ('stop hitting', 'reduce tantrums'). Instead they are positive targets of new skills that should help the child, such as early skills of negotiation and use of external mediators to cope with transitions.

Child:	Parents:
Teacher/practitioners:	
Child's strengths	
Intrinsic motivation/flow Regardless of behaviour, we will make sure the child...	
Relationship building Ways in which we will try to build the relationship, irrespective of behaviour	
Information collected about behaviour (observation, etc.)	
Initial hypothesis/unmet needs (Relatedness? Autonomy? Competence?)	
Ways we might help	
Child's target(s) *Positive, specific and achievable.*	

Figure P4.1 Proforma for preparing for meeting to discuss a child's behaviour

10

Planning for positive behaviour
Parents' viewpoints

Parents are a diverse group and it would be foolhardy to attempt any generalisations. The importance of keeping an open mind and avoiding hasty judgements cannot be over-emphasised. Self-fulfilling prophecies, where teachers form a negative judgement, and children and families 'live down' to it, are a real danger (Rosenthal and Jacobson 1968; Hauser-Cram et al. 2003; Rosenthal 2003). Effective work with parents involves establishing constructive dialogue (which includes careful listening) and maintaining a focus on what is helpful for the child. The Nigerian writer Chimamanda Adichie (online) talks powerfully about 'the danger of a single story' and reminds us about the complexity, richness and strengths that get lost when we resort to stereotypes. Practitioners need to be aware of the danger of colluding with stereotypes of 'uncaring', 'inadequate' or 'pushy' parents.

The association between poverty and poor outcomes for children (including behaviour problems) exists and it is important to acknowledge this when decisions have to be made in targeting scarce resources. However, the demonisation of sections of society through, for example, the government's use of the term 'troubled families' (DCLG 2012) is not constructive. Poverty certainly makes people's lives harder but it is not invariably associated with children who misbehave and underachieve. It is more likely that correlates of poverty, such as drug or alcohol dependence or other mental health problems, account for the link with poorer outcomes for children. Such problems may be less easily identified than poverty. Again, even in cases of severe mental illness that might interfere with bringing up children, families differ in the outcomes achieved as there may be protective and supportive factors in the wider family. Belsky (1984) promotes a model of parenting that considers not just the parents' personalities and psychological well-being but also the social support they enjoy and the characteristics of the child. While the research evidence suggests that all children can thrive, given optimal care, it also acknowledges that some babies' temperaments call for greater internal resources from adults. Furthermore, there is likely to be a question of 'goodness of fit' between children and adults, such that some pairings find it particularly hard to attune. Adults and children in this situation need help and support.

The focus of this book is on what adults can do to promote positive behaviour. Biological influences on behaviour have received less coverage. Increasingly, as indicated in Chapter 1, the complexities of the interaction between biology and environment are being unravelled but there is still much that is not fully understood. An informed approach should use research knowledge to formulate hypotheses about what behaviour might signify in terms of unmet needs and to draw up plans accordingly. The initial hypothesis is a 'best guess'. It might not lead to the hoped-for success and another hypothesis might then need to be considered and addressed. Parents should certainly not be blamed for a child's behaviour and the tentative nature of attempts to help should be acknowledged, with parents treated as partners in trying to formulate a plan of action.

We will now consider each of the psychological needs in turn and how settings might work with parents in ways that take account of the particular need under consideration. Readers may find it useful to consult the bullet points in the Introductions to the earlier parts of the book since they summarise the environments that are supportive or undermining for each of the psychological needs of relatedness, autonomy and competence.

Relatedness

- Settings need to be open with, and welcoming of, parents from their initial contact. Parents will come from a whole range of backgrounds and there may be some with little understanding of early years education and care in the UK. Some will have their own unfortunate memories of educational establishments. Many will be unfamiliar with the terminology of the EYFS (DfE 2014b) which practitioners may unwittingly use (e.g. 'doing his learning journey', 'my key group'). Practitioners should try to be friendly and clear without being condescending and should encourage parents to ask for clarification.

- Be informed about sources of support for families in the area and display literature relating to these. Find out as much about them as you can by visiting, talking to the professionals involved and/or to families from your setting who have used the service. If you build relationships with parents and suggest a particular service to them from a position of knowledge, there is a greater likelihood that they will access it than if they simply see a poster advertising the same service.

- Behaviour issues can be embarrassing for parents and other parents can ostracise a parent whose child is hurting others. Children in the UK are not legally obliged to attend school until the term following their fifth birthday. Some parents of children who display challenging behaviour withdraw the child from early education. This tends to compound any problems because the child then misses the opportunity to mix with other pre-schoolers and develop social and behavioural skills before school entry. Take a strong line in your behaviour policy about every child's right to a positive approach to any behavioural needs, assuring all parents that informed individual plans will be drawn up and implemented as necessary and that they should discuss any concerns with the manager. In some cases, managers have stamped out unhelpful muttering among parents by calling a meeting to explain that an action plan is in place and that trust and support from the community are expected in helping any child with needs (a manager doing this would have requested permission from the parent of the child whose behaviour is of concern, and observed due confidentiality).

- Aim for balance in the information shared with parents of a child with concerning behaviour. While incidents where others have been hurt must be shared, ensure you do not give just the 'bad news'. The child and parent are to be valued despite certain behaviour being unacceptable. Ways of demonstrating that value are likely to be individual to the case and it is important to reflect on this and do it in a meaningful way.

- If a parent seems to be struggling to have a positive view of their child, ask about exceptions to the negative picture: 'When is Harry usually at his most co-operative?', 'Are there times when you and Bethany have a lot of fun together?'

Autonomy

- Consider acknowledging the sensitivity of discussing a child's behaviour:

  'Behaviour can be such a sensitive topic, can't it? No parent wants to have to discuss how their child is hurting others. These things happen sometimes among young children and our interest is just in working with you to help Madison enjoy pre-school and get on well with the other children.'

- If the parent shares aspects of their experience, acknowledge what is going on in their lives: 'You were up most of the night with the baby, you must be exhausted', 'Your mother is still in hospital, what a worry'.

- Ask open-ended, non-judgemental questions to find out about behaviour issues and parents' feelings and attitudes: 'So, these "meltdowns", tell me about them. You say she had one yesterday. What provoked it?'

- Share ideas about what may be behind a child's behaviour in a tentative, blame-free manner and invite parents' comments. Remember that parents may have little to say when an idea is first floated but may go away and think about it. Try to 'touch base' with them again in the near future and invite any further comments/questions.

- When discussing the approach you are taking or plan to take, explain the underlying rationale and what you hope to achieve. Ask parents for ways that they think they can support the approach.

- Respect parents' choices.

- Sometimes practitioners feel strongly that parents need to seek medical or other advice about a child's behaviour. It is vital to advise parents to do this, when appropriate. Recognise, however, that taking such a step may feel to some parents like an admission that something is wrong, which in turn may trigger a grieving process for the loss of the 'perfect' child they expected. Most people know not to hurry grief after a death but may be less aware of the sensitivity sometimes required around surfacing developmental issues or possible problems in young children. Parents may need time to accept that their child may have particular needs. Practitioners often feel frustrated that parents delay giving permission for, or seeking, specialist advice that might help. Early years practitioners can also, sometimes unfairly, be blamed by schools for not having initiated earlier involvement of other professionals. Parents' rights must be respected and it is crucial to maintain relationships and make suggestions using a 'drip, drip' rather than a 'steamroller' approach.

- The reverse sort of case also occurs where practitioners feel that parents are too rapidly seeking a medical diagnosis for a child's behaviour rather than working in partnership to try to bring about positive change. It is important to listen to the parents' views and get the whole picture. People may see a diagnosis of some sort as an end in itself, whereas it is more of a signpost to approaches that might be helpful. Practitioners and parents can try relevant approaches with or without a diagnosis. Practitioners can respect parents' desire for a medical answer, while keeping a focus on practical changes that can be made to help the child.

Competency

- Using a 'story sack' approach, prepare information and resources that parents can borrow on a range of issues that link to behaviour such as 'Good nights – happy bedtime routines', 'A new baby', 'When someone close dies'. Each pack should include brief but research-informed information for adults, age-appropriate books and resources for adults and children to share and a list of relevant local organisations.

- Raising an issue about a child's behaviour almost invariably risks threatening a parent's sense of competence. When people feel threatened, they tend to become defensive and this can block open and constructive problem-solving. Take particular care not to criticise, particularly at the early stages of working with parents on their child's behaviour. Effective approaches start with noticing and commenting on positive aspects of parent–child interaction: 'It's lovely how she's always so pleased to see you when you collect her.' 'It's great that you are patient when she takes you round to see all the different things she has done.'

- If you invite parents in for extra meetings to discuss the child's behaviour, make sure they know what to expect – alert them if, for example, an Area

Special Needs Co-ordinator will be present or if you intend to complete some formal paperwork with them. Parents should always be welcome to bring a supporter along, whether a relative, friend or someone else. The main rule is not to spring surprises on people as this undermines competence in a situation where it is likely to be somewhat shaky anyway.

- Use every opportunity to model the type of interaction with the child that you consider most helpful.

- In making suggestions to help parents change their patterns of interaction with the child, bear in mind that it is important to empower them and not to overwhelm them. Discuss with them but also use your judgement to suggest changes that are achievable.

Case study: Angelika, 4 years old

The Special Educational Needs Co-ordinator (SENCo) has been asked to help draw up a behaviour plan for Angelika, a little girl who is frequently in clashes with other children and starts shouting and crying when they will not do what she wants. Angelika also sometimes creates a fuss about wanting to be first in a line. Although generally friendly with the adults, there are occasions when Angelika says 'No!' to their requests. The SENCo has carried out observations and prepared for a meeting with the parents and Pauline, the Key Person.

Child: Angelika, 4	Parents: Angie and Geoff

| Teacher/practitioners:
Pauline, Key Person | |

Child's strengths
Now settled well. Happy to play in a variety of areas and her achievements are at the level expected. She is articulate and has a wide vocabulary. Her physical skills (climbing, etc.) have really come on. She is socially oriented, lively and wants to play with others.

Intrinsic motivation/flow
Regardless of behaviour, we will make sure the child...
Continues to have access to all the play opportunities and everything available.

Relationship building
Ways in which we will try to build the relationship irrespective of behaviour
Pauline has a good relationship with A and will continue to have some individual chats with her every day.

Information collected about behaviour (observation, etc.)

Stormy disputes with other children that adults have to defuse. Sometimes refuses to do what adults ask (e.g. tidy up) and/or makes a huge fuss about being first in line.

Observation – key findings
- Some children seem to be avoiding playing with A. They move away when she goes to an area (scared?).
- About 50% joint play episodes pass peacefully and constructively.
- The incidents with adults seem to occur when A has already been upset by something else.

Initial hypothesis/unmet needs (Relatedness? Autonomy? Competence?)

Autonomy? Accepting boundaries? Relinquishing control at times?
Understanding others' emotions/perspectives and being able to compromise?

Ways we might help
(Whole group level/Changes in the physical environment/Changes in how adults react/Strategies to support the child (mediators?)
- Renewed emphasis on emotion coaching and inductive approaches with whole group.
- Puppet work with the whole group. Modelling listening to each other and joint problem solving. Being assertive in asking someone to listen. 'You want..., I want...What can we do?' Joint problem solving.
- Adults to model approach and wording with each other and to coach all the children in using the approach.
- Put up visual reminders of the wording so adults use the wording consistently.
- Adult to follow A to area and encourage children to stay and play with A, monitoring to ensure a positive experience for all.
- If there is a 'blow up' with other children:
  - build in some positive 1:1 time with Pauline once A is calm.
  - avoid confrontation when she may still be vulnerable to upset/ 'controlling' behaviour, e.g. sidestep the first in line problem by giving her a special job which she likes.

Child's target(s)	To pause when she is playing and
Positive, specific and achievable.	there is a disagreement. Ask the other child what they want. State what they each want: 'You want..., I want...What can we do?' *Provide coaching to begin with. Consider identifying a mediator.*

Figure 10.1 Preparation for meeting to discuss Angelika's behaviour

(Continued)

Through her observations, the SENCo thinks many of the disputes that Angelika has with adults could be avoided by noting when she clashes with other children and being aware of her increased susceptibility to enter into disputes with adults in the period shortly afterwards. The SENCo feels it may be possible to take preventative steps to minimise the likelihood of this chain of events. Her initial hypotheses about Angelika's behaviour with other children encompass issues to do with autonomy and control and issues related to understanding others' perspectives and finding compromises. The SENCo has generated some possible approaches that might help Angelika in particular while being beneficial for all the children.

Pauline has mentioned that Angelika's mother, Angie, is very uncomfortable at hearing about Angelika's behaviour. When Angelika's behaviour was first mentioned, Angie was both surprised and anxious. She commented: 'She's not like that at home' and 'I want her to be happy here – maybe it's not right for her'. Pauline asked how Angelika is with other children at home. Angie said she is fine with her friends' children and her cousin but they are all several years older. Pauline remembered that Angelika did not start nursery until she was $3\frac{1}{2}$ and that the settling-in period had been hard for both Angie and Angelika – particularly for Angie, she thought.

The SENCo has thus been alerted to Angie's sensitivities. She looks forward to meeting Angelika's father, as yet unknown to the staff. Both parents come and the meeting is intense and revealing. Angie's husband, Geoff, is older and tells them he was married previously when a very young man and has two sons, now grown-up. He says he was too young then and did not fully appreciate his boys or give them enough attention. They both talk with pride of Angelika. She was a premature baby born after in vitro fertilisation and needing weeks in the neonatal care unit. Angie becomes very emotional, talking of her 'miracle baby'. Geoff says: 'Angelika is Angie's world, she's our world. It looked like she might not make it through and now she's so bright – you said yourself how well she talks. Angie's done a great job with her.'

When they are asked about Angelika's experience with other children, Geoff says, 'Well, Angie's friends' children are all that bit older. That's what I was telling you, we had to wait and of course we didn't know if it would work out right in the end but it did and we got our little girl'. Pauline asks if Geoff's boys played together well as young kids. 'I think so, no worse than any others. But I wasn't there much, I worked long hours. Unfortunately those boys didn't get the time and attention Angelika does, that's my big regret.'

The discussion of the problems around Angelika's conception and birth is emotional and takes some time but the parents seem to want to share these details and the setting staff gain an insight into Angelika's status as a 'miracle baby' and how this may have affected how much control she experiences at home. Angelika mixes with older children when with her parents and they are probably more likely to allow her what she wants than are the peers at nursery. The SENCo asks Geoff and Angie if they would like to take a break now and whether they would be able to come back to continue the meeting in a couple of days' time. This suits everyone and so is agreed.

When the meeting resumes two days' later, there is a rapport between the parents and staff because of the emotions shared in the first meeting. The parents are less emotional now and ready to engage in problem-solving and constructive discussion regarding a plan to help Angelika. Geoff says he realised that Angelika has things her own way a lot but he hadn't seen that this could cause her problems. He comments that his boys had to learn to compromise and 'rub along' because they had little choice. Geoff can sees various issues at home, such as bedtimes, and thinks that change could be in everyone's interests. He and Angie talk about how little time they get together in the evenings because it is so hard to settle Angelika. Angie says she doesn't like rushing Angelika or leaving her at night when she wants more stories, a drink or something else because she wants Angelika to know how loved she is. Angie hadn't thought that it might be in Angelika's interests (as well as easier for them as parents) to be firmer about bedtime. Angie and Geoff agree some steps they will take to put in firmer boundaries at home. They are happy for the strategies that the SENCo suggests to be tried at the setting.

With the setting and parents working together, concerns about Angelika's behaviour decrease over time. Angelika, with her good verbal skills and social orientation, soon becomes adept and creative in proposing compromises! The first serious consultation with both parents over Angelika's behaviour took two relatively long meetings but the SENCo values the relationship formed with the parents through listening to their story and feels that the time has been invested well to promote partnership working.

11

Planning for positive behaviour
Practitioners' viewpoints

Practitioners working with children are in an extremely influential position. It seems a truism that meeting practitioners' psychological needs would boost performance in the interests of children. The success or otherwise of a research-based pedagogical approach is related to the fidelity with which the teacher uses the approach (Gresham et al. 1993). This in turn seems likely to be linked to the degree to which the teacher embraces and identifies with the approach, as opposed to being required to carry it out. In other words, teachers' perceived autonomy is important. Effective intervention involves working in partnership with practitioners (Power et al. 2005) and some of the most successful programmes, such as the Incredible Years Teacher Classroom Management Training (Webster-Stratton et al. 2011) take care to work collaboratively and supportively with teachers, meeting their needs for relatedness, autonomy and competence.

Just as behaviour is a sensitive and tricky issue for parents, the same can be true for practitioners. Those who work with young children generally enjoy their company and take pride in the warmth of the relationships they foster. Practitioners can be shocked and uncomfortable if a child's behaviour evokes strongly negative feelings. Their competence can be threatened if they feel unable to 'manage' a child using their usual strategies. Attitudes such as 'we shouldn't have to deal with this' can all too quickly prevail and block effective problem-solving.

In this chapter, we consider practitioners' needs for relatedness, autonomy and competence from the viewpoint of a manager or SENCo whose role is to manage and motivate staff to ensure children and families are appropriately supported. Again, readers may find it useful to consult the bullet points in the Introductions to the earlier parts of the book since they summarise the environments that are supportive or undermining for each of the three psychological needs.

Relatedness

- Settings and schools need to create an ethos where there are positive relationships between staff but where any member, regardless of age or amount of experience, can ask questions regarding practice and suggest changes. This should be part of how a setting operates, reflecting on practice and experimenting with change. Not all changes will prove beneficial and again this needs to be acknowledged and accepted, with no repercussions for someone who suggested a change that does not work. Managers need to be alert to cliques of staff who resist change and try to sabotage it. Open discussion in individual supervision should be used to guard against or tackle this.

- Another danger is that staff, mindful of the pressure a colleague is under because of a particular child's behaviour, support that colleague by agreeing that there is nothing more she can do and that the situation is untenable. This type of support runs the danger of becoming collusive and creating a barrier to positive change.

- Indicators of a healthy positive ethos in a setting might include:

  - Evidence that new approaches are regularly implemented and evaluated.

  - A 'Key Person' policy which states that there may be an occasional change in the allocated Key Person, in the interests of the child.

  - 'Debriefing' sessions offered to any member of staff coping with challenging behaviour.

Autonomy

- While it is important to avoid colluding with views engendered by the frustration of a colleague who is struggling, the feelings of such a colleague should be acknowledged. In Chapter 5 the purpose of emotions, including 'negative' ones, was discussed. Dreikurs (Dreikurs et al. 1971: 39) points out that practitioners' fleeting gut reactions to a child's behaviour are informative. He uses a different framework from that employed in this book, but it is possible to translate his ideas into the terminology used here (Table 11.1).

- A manager or SENCo can use Dreikur's ideas both to acknowledge a practitioner's feelings but also to discuss constructive ways forward. Note that the 'gut responses' to the feelings all feed into vicious cycles that are likely to amplify and perpetuate the unwanted behaviour. The adult's executive functions and professionalism are needed to break out of such cycles and to chart a more positive course, focused on the child's needs. 'Reframing' a situation that causes negative emotion, particularly anger, is one of the healthiest ways of managing the emotion (Goleman 1996; Mauss 2005).

- The adults working closely with a child, whether practitioners, teachers or teaching assistants need to be involved in devising any behaviour plan for a child. An external expert or a SENCo may usefully suggest certain approaches but, if a plan is to work, the adults responsible for it must understand and be in broad agreement with the approach and have some say in the details of its implementation. It is time-consuming to develop plans in this way but promoting autonomy in practitioners and parents is an investment as it increases the chances of effective change.

Table 11.1 Practitioners' gut reactions as indicators of children's unmet needs

Practitioner's 'gut reaction'	'Gut response'	Child's need
Annoyance/irritation 'It's non-stop. She never lets me get a sentence out or help anyone else without demanding attention'	Give 'negative' attention 'Jordan, stop interrupting'	Relatedness Secure, responsive, consistent care (The child is not secure enough)
Angry or threatened 'She just will not do as requested'	Increase demands (the vicious cycle of harsh undermining of autonomy – see Chapter 6)	Autonomy Opportunities for age-appropriate choice and 'power' within structured limits (The child may be reacting to repeated coercive experiences or to a scary lack of boundaries on behaviour and power)
Hurt 'I can't believe she did that after I've invested so much in building a relationship and things were going so much better'	Withdraw emotionally	Relatedness Unconditional acceptance (The child may distrust closeness, feeling unlovable)
Despair/hopelessness 'She just will not engage positively. There's nothing more I can do'	Give up, leave the child alone	Competence (The child feels incapable and hopeless)

Source: Based on Dreikurs (1971).

Competence

- Practitioners need opportunities to continue to learn about children's needs and approaches for meeting them. If they are working with a child with a known or suspected learning difference (for example, an autistic spectrum difference or an attention and hyperactivity difference), they are likely to benefit from opportunities to learn more. Training courses, reading and visits to settings that have developed expertise in helping children with similar needs can all be helpful.

- If a member of staff already has experience of the approach under consideration, provide opportunities for that person to work alongside the practitioner with less experience, modelling the approach with the child and coaching the colleague.

- Managers and SENCos have a useful role to play in helping a practitioner prioritise how to implement any new ideas, ensuring that changes are manageable and staggered if necessary.

Case study: Ethan, 5 years old

Ethan has just started school, having previously attended a Montessori nursery where he was settled. The transition to school has been very difficult and he seems very agitated, anxious and unable to meet the expectations of being part of a group. The SENCo has become involved and has carried out some observations. He is still trying to unravel the complexities of Ethan's needs. His initial ideas are recorded in his planning for a meeting with parents and staff.

Child: Ethan 5½	Parents: Mr and Mrs White
Teacher/practitioners: Tamsin Green, teacher Hilary, teaching assistant	
Child's strengths Wonderful Duplo construction and advanced language for thinking displayed while working on it.	
Intrinsic motivation/flow *Regardless of behaviour, we will make sure the child...* Has uninterrupted opportunities each day to carry out an activity of his choice (likely to be Duplo or other constructional materials).	

Relationship building
Ways in which we will try to build the relationship irrespective
of behaviour
See below. Ethan seems to benefit from a low-key, indirect approach. All
   staff to try this and Hilary, teaching assistant, to try to continue to give
   him some 1:1 time each day.	

(Continued)

Information collected about behaviour (observation, etc.)
- Hiding under the table – happening every day – for up to 2 hours at a time.
- Does not seem to see himself as part of a group. Gets agitated when he is expected to do things with other children or when other children are very close to him. This often seems to be when he goes under a table.
- He appears to shrink from direct eye contact and being in the spotlight. The teaching assistant will hunker down behind him sometimes when he is under the table and say a few things to him calmly and quietly. He seems to be beginning to trust her but any relationship is developing slowly.

Initial hypothesis/unmet needs (Relatedness? Autonomy? Competence?)
Relatedness? Check parents' views on his relationships. Has there been any trauma? How would they describe him as a baby?
Competence and communication, particularly social pragmatic communication?
Anxiety – could have various roots. Would greater predictability and warning of transitions and of expectations help?

Ways we might help
(*Whole group level /Changes in the physical environment/Changes in how adults react/Strategies to support the child (mediators?)*)
- Look at the timetable and try to reduce the demands on E for group activities in the short term. Make him his own visual timetable and encourage him to consult it before and after each activity. Build in some choice in the order of activities.
- Warn him some time before transitions and see if he would find an egg timer helpful.
- Be sensitive to his need for physical and psychological space and talk to him without demanding eye contact and in a fairly 'low-key' manner.
- Regard going under the table as a retreat to a safe place and do not immediately challenge this choice. After 5–10 minutes of self-selected 'time out', invite him to re-join activities.

Child's target(s) *Positive, specific and achievable.*	• Use personal timetable and follow one transition successfully each day. • Successfully use a 5-minute sand timer to transition from one activity to another.

Figure 11.1 Preparation for meeting to discuss Ethan's behaviour

The SENCo sees this as a complex case where both the parents' and the teacher's feelings could become a barrier to moving the situation forward. He is interested in the fact that Ethan attended a Montessori nursery and was not flagged up as presenting any behavioural challenges. He realises he needs to handle matters sensitively with all concerned to maximise the chances of effective joint working. He prepares for the meeting with parents particularly carefully, almost preparing a script using the meeting format.

SENCo's notes for meeting about Ethan

- Welcome and introductions
- E's strengths – I observed him building a wonderful construction from Duplo and he displayed complex language for thinking when talking about it.
- Sorry that E's start has not been as smooth as we all would have hoped. Can you tell us what it has been like from your point of view? (How this behaviour relates to previous behaviour? What do they make of the problems? What might help? If they talk about E not displaying behavioural problems at the Montessori nursery, ask what features of that provision seemed to suit him?)
- Invite Tamsin (teacher) and Hilary (TA) to outline behaviour they have observed and their attempts to help.
- Relationships. E can talk well about a task he is involved in but he is relatively unresponsive to general conversation and interaction. In fact he seems to shy away from it. Was he interactive as a baby? What is he like with you? How is he with family and friends?
- Unless other ideas emerge more strongly, suggest that E needs help to manage anxiety, understand social expectations and to follow the routines and structure.

Invite suggestions about ways to achieve this involving everyone.

Include the suggestions from the proforma – but only if everyone thinks they are workable.

- Possible target(s) for E? (as in proforma if they still seem appropriate).
- Check for additional comments/ideas.
- Thank all for coming. Assure parents of availability tomorrow if they have further ideas on reflection. Would they like a telephone call to touch base?

A final, but crucial, part of the SENCo's preparation for chairing the meeting with parents is to have an informal discussion with the teacher. Tamsin Green has been teaching for three years and is a warm teacher, popular with children, parents and her colleagues. She has tried very hard to form a relationship with Ethan, talking to him and often smiling at him but he turns away and there is no positive response. The SENCo wonders if Tamsin's attempts to be friendly might be having the opposite effect to that she intends, making Ethan more wary of her. Ethan hides under the table regularly and Tamsin tries to coax him out, to no effect. She has also tried telling him to come out using a firm voice but Ethan stays put. The SENCo recognises that the situation with Ethan is the greatest challenge Tamsin has faced so far in terms of forming a relationship with a child in her class. The SENCo has noticed that this normally caring and warm teacher

(Continued)

is beginning to talk in terms of 'something wrong' with Ethan, rather than 'ways to help' him. He realises he will need to work hard to keep Tamsin on board as part of the solution to the situation.

The SENCo arranges to see Tamsin and, over tea and biscuits, encourages the young teacher to talk about the uncomfortable feelings that Ethan is engendering in her. He says to Tamsin that the cocktail of hurt, hopelessness and anger she is experiencing is a testament to how much she has tried to build a relationship with Ethan and to encourage him to meet behavioural expectations. The SENCo says these feelings are what he would expect from a passionate, caring teacher. The SENCo admits he is still puzzling over what to make of Ethan but points out that Tamsin's feelings might be saying something about Ethan's needs. Tamsin feels rejected by him and this might mean either that Ethan is distrustful because of rejection experiences in his past or that he cannot really understand relationships and is baffled and may be anxious about attempts to form them. The SENCo comments that a child who hides under tables for extensive periods is not a happy child and needs support. He says he is not sure how best to understand Ethan but is struck by his relationship difficulties, his anxiety and rigidity. They will need to meet his parents and then formulate a plan. The SENCo says he is sorry that Tamsin is struggling with the situation and that part of the plan for Ethan will include regular 'debriefings' for Tamsin and her teaching assistant where, among other things, they can express their feelings in a safe and confidential environment. For the meeting with Ethan's parents, though, the SENCo states that he is confident he can rely on Tamsin to be her usual factual and positive self.

In the meeting, the SENCo uses his prepared notes to lead the meeting but takes care to draw out the parents' views and to include everyone in the planning. He describes his observations. Tamsin pre-empts one of the SENCo's own ideas by saying, 'Ethan might find it easier if I'm less bouncy and "Tiggerish" when I talk to him'. The SENCo feels that Tamsin is fully on board again and that the extra meeting with her was worthwhile.

Ethan's parents describe him as 'self-contained' and acknowledge that he thrives on routine and needs time for individual, uninterrupted activity. At home he is no problem but he dislikes anything that breaks normal routines. They feel the individual approach at the Montessori nursery was helpful for him, as was the generous amount of physical space. They know school is making him anxious and support the ideas of an individual visual timetable and warning of transitions. At home they have quite set routines (for example, the same sequence of meals every week and set times for visiting grandparents) because this works best for Ethan. One of Ethan's older cousins has been diagnosed as having Asperger's syndrome and they say that they hoped Ethan was fine but they have used some of the strategies Mrs White's sister finds good for the cousin diagnosed with Asperger's syndrome because they found them useful. The SENCo does not pursue the question of a possible diagnosis for Ethan at this stage but says that the school will monitor how he reacts to the behaviour plan they put in place and the dialogue with the family will continue.

After the parents have gone, Tamsin says she knows little about Asperger's syndrome but would be interested in learning more. This the SENCo also sees as a positive indication of Tamsin's constructive interest in Ethan and he promises to pass her some relevant literature, thinking that she will feel more competent for informing herself. He stresses that she should avoid diagnosis and concentrate on understanding which strategies might help and why.

Appendix 1

Format for meeting with parents

Meeting format

- Thank attendees for coming, particularly parents.
- Introductions.
- Purpose: to share information about (child's name)'s behaviour with a view to drawing on everyone's views to find things we might be able to do to help.
- Pleased to have (child's name), outline strengths. Put behaviour in context (e.g. 'quite rare but still concerning', a couple of times a week which, while concerning means there are more days that are fine than not').
- Ask parents 'How are you feeling about (child's name) at nursery?' How is (child's name) at home? If relevant: and why do you think there is a difference?
- Outline the concerns, giving information from observations.
- Suggest initial hypothesis, appropriately worded.
- Invite comments.
- Revise or refine hypothesis in the light of the discussion.
- Suggest ideas about ways forward:
  - whole group level;
  - changes in the physical environment;
  - changes in how adults react;
  - strategies to support the child (**mediators**?);
  - positive target for child.
- Ask for ways parents can help.
- Ask for additional suggestions or modifications to suggestions.

- Stress that you will be providing positive experiences for the child not contingent on behaviour (and be prepared to justify).
- Agree review arrangements.
- Thank everyone for coming. Indicate availability for parents in the coming days after they have had a chance to reflect on the meeting. Would they appreciate a phone call?

Appendix 2

Proforma for preparing for meeting to discuss a child's behaviour

Child:	Parents:
Teacher/practitioners:	
Child's strengths	
Intrinsic motivation/flow Regardless of behaviour, we will make sure the child …	
Relationship building Ways in which we will try and build the relationship, irrespective of behaviour	
Information collected about behaviour (observation, etc.)	
Initial hypothesis/unmet needs (Relatedness? Autonomy? Competence?)	
Ways we might help	
Child's target(s) *Positive, specific and achievable.*	

Figure A2.1 Proforma for preparing for meeting to discuss a child's behaviour

Glossary

Glossary words are shown in bold on their first occurrence in the text.

Attachment bond – the emotional tie between two people. The first and most important attachment bonds are between and baby and the main carer(s).

Behavioural learning theory (behaviourism) – a school of psychology which looks at the external and the measurable, at behaviour rather than cognitions or feelings. The ways stimuli are presented and the effects that follow behaviours (contingencies) influence learning in specifiable ways (for example, behaviours that are rewarded tend to be repeated).

Contingent reward – a reward of the type 'do x and you will be rewarded by y'. The reward is usually presumed to increase the likelihood of someone doing x. When an activity is intrinsically rewarding, the addition of a contingent reward can dent motivation in the medium to long term.

Correlation – when there is a demonstrated relationship between two (or more) factors, they correlate. An example is that responsive, attuned caregiving correlates with secure attachment. A correlation does not necessarily indicate that one factor causes the other.

Differential susceptibility – this is the idea that individual differences that have tended to be associated with less good outcomes may not always result in these. There are some indications that characteristics that in suboptimal environments are considered risk factors may actually be positive characteristics in more favourable environments, resulting in better-than-average outcomes.

Early Years Foundation Stage (EYFS) – the statutory standards for the learning, development and care of children from birth to 5 years old in England. All schools and Ofsted-registered early years providers must follow the EYFS, including childminders, pre-schools, nurseries and school reception classes.

Elaborative talk – talk that goes beyond description and explores reasons. Elaborative talk by an adult helps a child to understand events in context and to evaluate them. It also supports memory of events.

Empirical evidence – evidence from experiments.

Executive functions – an umbrella term for a group of skills that require effort such as paying attention, planning, waiting and managing impulses. Executive functions are needed for any behaviour that goes beyond reacting to immediate stimuli.

Experiment – a well-designed experiment controls all variables other than the one being investigated and thus is the gold standard for establishing cause and effect. Sometimes questions can be raised about whether effects found in experiments discover the way things operate in the 'real world' where so many more influences may come into play.

Experimental paradigm – a particular model or way of carrying out an experiment. It is often challenging to design an ethical experiment that can be done with people and will illuminate what is really of interest. Innovative experimental paradigms often represent a step forward for research.

Externalising behaviour – a term used to refer to problematic 'acting out' behaviour directed against other people or against things, such as angry outbursts and aggression.

Humanist/humanism – humanists stress the value of each individual and their capacity to find a constructive route in life. Abraham Maslow is a famous humanist, best known for his hierarchy of needs which emphasises that, in optimum environments, humans strive for self-actualisation. Carl Rogers is another famous humanist who argued that children need unconditional love in order to thrive. The Deci and Ryan (2000) model that provides the framework for this book is in the humanist tradition.

Hypothesis – an informed guess that is then put to the test. An initial hypothesis will often be revised in the light of the findings from testing it. A process of hypothesis formulation and testing can be used as a means of helping children whose behaviour gives rise for concern.

Inductive socialisation or discipline – a style of interaction that provides reasons and explanations for the behavioural standards expected.

Internal representations – the rules and expectations that we hold inside ourselves. As children develop, they become less reliant on immediate stimuli or on support from people either prompting their prosocial behaviour or telling them what to do. They have built internal representations of how to behave.

Internal working models – mental representations. The term captures the fact that based on their experience, children will form expectations. Some children's working model will be positive (for example, 'The world is a friendly place and people will help me'), others will have much less positive ones (for example, 'I need to grab things and look after myself as much as possible, no one else can be relied on to ensure I get the things I need').

Internalisation – a natural developmental process whereby children build internal models of their world and how it works and the demands on them. When children have internalised the demands on them in a healthy manner, they agree with the importance and value of the things they have to do and do them willingly most of the time. With 'controlled' internalisation, the picture is less healthy. The child behaves from fear, from duty or a desire to retain love – though the behaviour may appear 'good', the child feels like a puppet on a string. Controlled internalisation puts children under strain and inter- feres with the development of autonomy.

Internalised behaviour difficulties – behaviour that is problematic and directed against the self. In the extreme this includes self-harming behav- iour or eating disorders. Very high levels of anxiety, social withdrawal and an extremely poor self-image are other examples.

Intrinsic motivation – motivation that comes from within and is not depend- ent on external recognition or rewards. Intrinsically motivated activities are those that someone chooses to do for the pleasure involved in doing them.

Joint attention – when adult and child share attention to an object, for exam- ple, when a child looks to see what the adult is looking at or when a child directs the adult's attention to an object by pointing towards it.

Key Person – it is a statutory requirement in England that a child attending a childcare and education setting be allocated a Key Person. This is in recogni- tion of the importance of attachment. The Key Person's most important role is to form a close relationship with the child and the family.

Leading activity – a term from Vygotskian psychology, the leading activity for a developmental level is the one which will have the most impact for development.

Longitudinal study – in a longitudinal study, researchers follow children over time and continue to collect data. Some longitudinal studies have followed children well into adulthood. Studying the same children over time provides much richer and often more meaningful information than do studies con- ducted at a single point in time. Longitudinal studies may indicate the long- term effects of particular strategies or factors.

Mediator – a Vygotskian term for an object that helps a child regulate an aspect of behaviour.

Mental state talk – talking that refers to what people feel, think, know, remem- ber and believe.

Mental tools ('tools of the mind') – a Vygotskian term to describe the men- tal processes that children develop which enable them to direct their own learning and behaviour rather than just being at the mercy of immediate environmental influences. The tools of the mind are culturally determined. Language is one of the most powerful tools of the mind.

Meta-emotion philosophy – one's general belief system about feelings and emotions and the degree to which they should be accorded importance.

Mind-minded – a term to describe adults whose behaviour indicates that they take account of children's minds, for example, they notice and correctly interpret and comment on a pre-verbal child's reactions.

Mindset – an internalised set of ideas through which people interpret their expe- riences. Dweck (2008) contrasts a growth mindset (where effort can always take one forward) with a fixed mindset (where a ceiling on achievement is perceived, despite effort).

Motherese – the way people naturally tend to talk to babies in a singsong voice, exaggerating certain words and using a high pitch. Motherese helps infants' language development. It is also referred to as infant-directed speech.

Naturalistic study – in a naturalistic study, the researcher aims to observe and record what happens in the natural environment, such as among family members at home or children within a childcare setting. Carefully collected and analysed data may reveal patterns. This method overcomes the problem of artificiality that can be levelled at experimental studies but findings are usually correlational, with assumptions made about causality.

Person praise – praise that is directed towards a person's (fixed) qualities rather than the person's actions, e.g. 'you're a good boy', 'what a clever girl'.

Primary attachment figure – the most important attachment figure for a baby, usually the mother.

Private (or egocentric) speech – speech that is communication with oneself rather than with someone else. Private speech is seen in Vygotskian theory as a significant step towards self-regulation of behaviour.

Process praise – praise that focuses on the effort a person has put in or the strategies used.

Prosocial – prosocial behaviour is deliberately aimed at helping others. It includes behaviours such as sharing, comforting and helping. Its opposite is anti-social behaviour.

Protoconversations – early interactions between adult and child before the child has acquired verbal language. Protoconversations have many features of conversation such as shared interest, eye contact and taking turns.

School readiness – a term that has become controversial because of a perceived emphasis on academic skills to make children 'ready for school'. There is a significant body of informed opinion that the onus should be on schools to be ready for and welcoming of children.

Secondary attachment figure – in addition to the strong attachment to the primary attachment figure(s) – usually the parent(s) – a child can form attachments to others, the secondary attachment figure(s). A Key Person with whom a child forms a warm bond would be a secondary attachment figure.

Secure base – for a child who has formed secure attachments, the attachment figures provide a secure base from which to explore. The child can wander a short distance and explore, knowing that the attachment figure will be there for attention and love when needed.

Self-determination – a healthy form of motivation in which people feel in charge of their own behaviour and that they have chosen it of their own free will. Deci and Ryan's (2000) self-determination theory holds that people feel self-determined when their needs for relatedness, autonomy and competence are met.

Sensitive period – a period when a particular aspect of development occurs most easily and naturally, given the right conditions.

Social (pragmatic) communication – a successful conversation requires more than comprehension of, and response to, the words said. The social (pragmatic) aspects are both non-verbal and verbal. They include cueing the listener into the topic, taking turns, responding to the topic or signalling a change of topic. Respecting the conversational partner's personal space and taking account of the status of the partner (addressing a head teacher differently from a peer) are further examples.

Social referencing – when children look to their attachment figures for cues which then inform their action, this is known as social referencing. A child interested in venturing a bit further away from the picnic group might look towards her mother, and remain where she is if her mother looks anxious but explore further if her mother smiles reassuringly.

Socialisation – the processes by which children absorb and learn about the typical patterns of social behaviour in the communities of which they are a part. Parents and practitioners are 'socialising agents' whose role can be construed as providing environments to facilitate children's motivation and responsibility.

Sociocultural theories – theorists in the sociocultural tradition stress the influence of society and culture on an individual's development. Society and culture includes any grouping that impacts on a child, for example, family, school, faith group, sports or other activity groups and the wider culture. Vygotsky is the 'father' of sociocultural theories. Bronfenbrenner's ecological systems theory can also be seen to fit within this tradition.

'Strange situation' – an experimental set-up designed by Mary Ainsworth to gauge an infant's attachment style by seeing a child's behaviour with a stranger during brief absences of the mother and how the child responds when the mother returns.

Systems approach – an approach that does not consider individuals in isolation but within the various systems they are part of, such as family systems, wider social systems and school systems.

Theory – a coherent set of ideas formulated to provide an underlying explanation of phenomena and to predict further phenomena.

Theory of Mind – the understanding that people inhabit mental worlds and that different people can have different beliefs, intentions and desires.

Unconditional positive regard – considering someone as of worth whatever they do. A person's behaviour need not be approved but the person can still be highly valued.

Zone of proximal development – the area of learning just beyond what the child can currently achieve independently but where support from a more knowledgeable other will enable him or her to achieve more.

References

Adamson, L. and Frick, J. (2003) The Still-Face: a history of a shared experimental paradigm, *Infancy*, 4(4): 451–73.

Adichie, C. (n.d.) TED talk: the danger of a single story. Available at: www.ted.com/talks/chimamanda_adichie_the_danger_of_a_single_story (accessed 19 August 2014).

Ainsworth, M.D.S. (1978) *Patterns of Attachment: A Psychological Study of the Strange Situation*. Hillsdale, NJ: Erlbaum.

Ainsworth, M.D.S. and Bell, S.M. (1970) Attachment, exploration and separation: illustrated by the behavior of one-year-olds in a strange situation, *Child Development*, 41: 49–67.

Ainsworth, M.D.S. and Marvin, R.S. (1995) On the shaping of a theory and research: an interview with Mary D.S. Ainsworth (Fall 1994), *Monographs of the Society for Research in Child Development*, 60(2/3): 3–21.

Allen, G. (2011) *Early Intervention: The Next Steps. An Independent Report to Her Majesty's Government*, Available at: http://media.education.gov.uk/assets/files/pdf/g/graham%20allens%20review%20of%20early%20intervention.pdf (accessed 2 February 2012).

Bakermans-Kranburg, M., van IJzendoorn, M. and Juffer, F. (2003) Less is more: meta-analyses of sensitivity and attachment interventions in early childhood, *Psychological Bulletin*, 129: 195–215.

Baumeister, R.F., Campbell, J.D., Krueger, J.I. and Vohs, K.D. (2003) Does high self-esteem cause better performance, interpersonal success, happiness or healthier lifestyles? *Psychological Science in the Public Interest*, 4(1): 1–44.

Baumrind, D. (1966) Effects of authoritative parental control on child behaviour, *Child Development*, 37(4): 887–907.

Belsky, J. (1984) The determinants of parenting: a process model, *Child Development*, 5: 83–96.

Belsky, J., Bakermans-Kranenburg, M.J. and Van Ijzendoorn, M.H. (2007) For better *and* for worse: differential susceptibility to environmental influences, *Current Directions in Psychological Science*, 16: 300–4.

Bergen, D. and Mauer, D. (2000) Symbolic play, phonological awareness and literacy skills at three age levels, in K.A. Roskos and J.F. Christie (eds) *Play and Literacy in Early Childhood: Research from Multiple Perspectives*. New York: Erlbaum.

Berkman, L.F. and Glass, T. (2000) Social integration, social networks, social support, and health, in L.F. Berkman and I. Kawachi (eds) *Social Epidemiology*. New York: Oxford University Press.

Bierman, K.L., Nix, R.L., Greenberg M.T. et al. (2008) Executive functions and school readiness intervention: impact, moderation, and mediation in the Head Start REDI program, *Development and Psychopathology*, 20: 821–43.

Blakemore, S.-J. and Frith, U. (2005) *The Learning Brain: Lessons for Education*. Oxford: Blackwell Publishing.

Bodrova, E. and Leong, D.J. (2007) *Tools of the Mind. The Vygotskian Approach to Early Childhood Education*, 2nd edn, Upper Saddle River, NJ: Pearson Merrill/Prentice Hall.

Bowlby, J. (1966) *Maternal Care and Mental Health. A Report Prepared on Behalf of the World Health Organization as a Contribution to the United Nations Programme for the Welfare of Homeless Children*. New York: Schocken.

Bowlby, J. (2005) *The Making and Breaking of Affectional Bonds*. London: Routledge Classics.

Bradbury, B.M., Corak, J., Waldfogel, J. and Washbrook, E. (2012) Inequality in early child outcomes, in J. Ermisch, M. Jäntti and T. Smeeding (eds) *From Parents to Children: The Intergenerational Transmission of Advantage*. New York: Russell Sage Foundation.

Bretherton, I. (1992) The origins of attachment theory: John Bowlby and Mary Ainsworth, *Developmental Psychology*, 28: 759–75.

Bretherton, I. (2010) Fathers in attachment theory and research: a review, *Early Child Development and Care*, 180(1–2): 9–23.

Bronson, P. and Merryman, A. (2010) *Nurture Shock*. Reading: Ebury Press.

Brown, J.R., Donelan-McCall, N. and Dunn, J. (1996) Why talk about mental states? The significance of children's conversations with friends, siblings and mothers, *Child Development*, 67(3): 836–49.

Chorpita, B.F. and Barlow, D.H. (1998) The development of anxiety: the role of control in the early environment, *Psychological Bulletin*, 124(1): 3–21.

Corpus, H.J. and Lepper, M.R. (2007) The effect of person versus performance praise on children's motivation: gender and age as moderating factors, *Educational Psychology*, 27(4): 487–508.

Csikszentmihalyi, M. (1975) *Beyond Boredom and Anxiety. Experiencing Flow in Work and Play*. San Francisco, CA: Jossey-Bass.

Cutting, A.L. and Dunn, J. (2006) Conversations with siblings and with friends: links between relationship quality and social understanding, *British Journal of Developmental Psychology*, 24: 73–87.

David, T., Goouch, K., Powell, S. and Abbott, L. (2003) *Birth to Three Matters: A Review of the Literature*. London: Department for Education and Skills.

DCLG (Department for Communities and Local Government) (2012) *Helping Troubled Families Turn Their Lives Around*. Available at: https://www.gov.uk/government/policies/helping-troubled-families-turn-their-lives-around (accessed 31 October 2014).

Deci, E.L. and Ryan, R.M. (2000) The 'what' and 'why' of goal pursuits: human needs and the self-determination of behaviour, *Psychological Inquiry*, 11(4): 227–68.

Deci, E.L. and Ryan, R.M. (2002) *The Handbook of Self-Determination Research*. Rochester, NY: University of Rochester Press.

Dettling, A., Gunnar, M. and Donzella, B. (1999) Cortisol levels of young children in full-day childcare settings, *Psychoneuroendocrinology*, 24: 519–36.

DfE (Department for Education) (2012) *Statutory Framework for the Early Years Foundation Stage 2012*. Available at: http://webarchive.nationalarchives.gov.uk/20130401151715/ https://www.education.gov.uk/publications/standard/allpublications/page1/ dfe-00023-2012 (accessed 20 October 2014).

DfE (Department for Education) (2013) *Working Together to Safeguard Children*. Available at: https://www.gov.uk/government/publications/working-together-to-safeguard-children (accessed 25 October 2014).

DfE (Department for Education) (2014a) *Permanent and Fixed-Period Exclusions in England, 2012–2013*. Available at: www.gov.uk/government/statistics/permanent-and-fixed-period-exclusions-in-england-2012-to-2013 (accessed 25 August 2014).

DfE (Department for Education) (2014b) *Statutory Framework for the Early Years Foundation Stage: Setting the Standards for Learning, Development and Care for Children from Birth to Five*. Available at: http://www.foundationyears.org.uk/ eyfs-statutory-framework/ (accessed 20 October 2014).

DfES (Department for Education and Skills) (2007) *The Early Years Foundation Stage: Setting the Standards for Learning, Development and Care for Children from Birth to Five*. Nottingham: DfES Publications.

Diamond, A. (2013) Executive functions, *Annual Review of Psychology*, 64: 135–68.

Diamond, A. and Lee, K. (2011) Interventions shown to aid executive function development in children 4–12 years old, *Science*, 333: 956–64.

Diener, C.I. and Dweck, C.S. (1978) An analysis of learned helplessness: continuous changes in performance, strategy and achievement cognitions following failure, *Journal of Personality and Social Psychology*, 36: 451–62.

Dix, T., Stewart, A.D., Gershoff, E.T. and Day, W.H. (2007) Autonomy and children's reactions to being controlled: evidence that both compliance and defiance may be positive markers in early development, *Child Development*, 78(4): 1204– 21.

Dreikurs, R., Grunwald, B.B. and Pepper, F.C. (1971) *Maintaining Sanity in the Classroom: Illustrated Teaching Techniques*. London: Harper and Row.

Dunn, J. (1988) *The Beginnings of Social Understanding*. Cambridge, MA: Harvard University Press.

Dunn, J. (2004) *Children's Friendships: The Beginnings of Intimacy*. Oxford: Blackwell.

Dunn, J., Brown, J. and Beardsall, L. (1991) Family talk about feeling states and children's later understanding of others' emotions, *Developmental Psychology*, 27(3): 448–55.

Dweck, C.S. (2000) *Self-Theories. Their Role in Motivation, Personality and Development*. Hove: Psychology Press.

Dweck, C.S. (2008) *Mindset: The New Psychology of Success*. New York: Ballantine Books.

Dweck, C.S. (2013) Social development, in P.D. Zelazo (ed.) *The Oxford Handbook of Developmental Psychology*, vol. 2: *Self and Other*. Available at: http://www.oxfordhandbooks.com/view/10.1093/oxfordhb/9780199958474.001.0001/oxfordhb-9780199958474-e-008?rskey=bRvHVS&result=2 (accessed 30 July 2014).

Dweck, C.S., Davidson, W., Nelson, S. and Enna, B. (1978) Sex differences in learned helplessness: I Differential debilitation with peer and adult evaluators, *Developmental Psychology*, 14: 258–78.

Early Education supported by the Department for Education (2012) *Development Matters in the Early Years Foundation Stage (EYFS)*. London: Early Education.

Ensor, R. and Hughes, C. (2005) More than talk: relations between emotion understanding and positive behaviour in toddlers, *British Journal of Developmental Psychology*, 23: 343–63.

Evangelou, M., Sylva, K., Kyriacou, M. et al. (2009) *Early Years Learning and Development. Literature Review. Research Report DCSF-RR176*. London: Department for Children, Schools and Families.

Galyer, K.T. and Evans, I.M. (2001) Pretend play and the development of emotion regulation in preschool children, *Early Child Development and Care*, 166(1): 93–108.

Gerhardt, S. (2004) *Why Love Matters: How Affection Shapes a Baby's Brain*. Hove: Brunner-Routledge.

Goldschmied, E. and Jackson, S. (2004) *People Under Three: Young Children in Day Care*, 2nd edn. London: Routledge.

Goleman, D. (1996) *Emotional Intelligence. Why It Can Matter More Than IQ*. London: Bloomsbury.

Gopnik, A, Meltzoff, A and Kuhl, P (2001) *How Babies Think*. London: Orion.

Goswami, U. and Bryant, P. (2007) *Children's Cognitive Development and Learning* (Primary Review Research Survey 2/1a), Cambridge: University of Cambridge Faculty of Education.

Gottman, J., with Declaire, J. (1997) *The Heart of Parenting. How to Raise an Emotionally Intelligent Child*. London: Bloomsbury.

Gottman, J.M., Katz, L.F. and Hooven, C. (1996) Parental meta-emotion philosophy and the emotional life of families: theoretical models and preliminary data, *Journal of Family Psychology*, 10(3): 243–68.

Gralinski, J.H. and Kopp, C.B. (1993) Everyday rules for behavior: mothers' requests to young children, *Developmental Psychology*, 29(3): 573–84.

Gray, C. (2001) *My Social Stories Book*. London: Jessica Kingsley Publishers.

Greenberg, M.T., Kusche, C.A., Cook, E.T. and Quamma, J.P. (1995) Promoting emotional competence in school-aged children: the effects of the PATHS curriculum, *Development and Psychopathology*, 7: 117–36.

Gresham, F.M., Gansle, K.A., Noell, G.H. et al. (1993) Treatment integrity of school-based behavioral intervention studies: 1980–1990, *School Psychology Review*, 22: 254–72.

Grieshaber, S.J. and McArdle, F. (2010) *The Trouble with Play*. Maidenhead: Open University Press.

Grossmann, K., Grossmann, K.E., Kindler, H. and Zimmermann, P. (2008) A wider view of attachment and exploration: the influence of mothers and fathers on the development of psychological security from infancy to young adulthood, in J. Cassidy and P.R. Shaver (eds) *Handbook of Attachment: Theory, Research and Clinical Applications*, 2nd edn. New York: Guilford Press.

Gunderson, E.A., Gripshover, S.J., Romero, C. et al. (2013) Parent praise to 1- to 3-year-olds predicts children's motivational frameworks 5 years later, *Child Development*, 84(5): 1526–41.

Gunnar, M.R. (1978) Changing a frightening toy into a pleasant toy by allowing the infant to control its actions, *Developmental Psychology*, 14(2): 157–62.

Gunnar, M.R. (1980) Control, warning signals and distress in infancy, *Developmental Psychology*, 16(4): 281–89.

Gunnar, M.R., Larson, M.C., Hertsgaard, L. et al. (1992) The stressfulness of separation among nine-month-old infants: effects of social context variables and infant temperament, *Child Development*, 63(2): 290–303.

Hammond, C. (2011) Mind changers: Walter Mischel's marshmallow study, BBC Radio 4. Available at: http://www.bbc.co.uk/programmes/b00ymjpr (accessed 15 September 2014).

Harris, P.L. (2006) Use your words, *British Journal of Developmental Psychology*, 24: 253–61.

Harris, P.L., de Rosnay, M. and Pons, F. (2005) Language and children's understanding of mental states, *Current Directions in Psychological Science*, 14: 69–73.

Hart, B. and Risley, T.R. (1995) *Meaningful Differences*. London: Brooks Publishing.

Hauser-Cram,P., Sirin, S.R. and Stipek, D. (2003) When teachers' and parents' values differ: teachers' ratings of academic competence in children from low-income families, *Journal of Educational Psychology*, 95(4): 813–20.

Hooper, J. (2012) *What Children Need to Be Happy, Confident and Successful: Step by Step Positive Psychology to Help Children Flourish*. London: Jessica Kingsley.

Hughes, C. and Dunn, J. (2000) Hedonism or empathy? Hard-to-manage children's moral awareness, and links with cognitive and maternal characteristics, *British Journal of Developmental Psychology*, 18: 227–45.

Hughes, C. and Dunn, J. (2002) When I say a naughty word: a longitudinal study of young children's accounts of anger in themselves and close others, *British Journal of Developmental Psychology*, 20(4): 515–35.

Humphrey, N. (1976) The social function of intellect, in P.P.G. Bateson and R.A. Hinde (eds) *Growing Points in Ethology*. Cambridge: Cambridge University Press.

Jack, R., Garrod, O. and Schyns, P. (2014) Dynamic facial expressions of emotion transmit an evolving hierarchy of signals over time, *Current Biology*, 24(2): 187–92.

Jogulekar, A. (2012) Chocolate consumption and Nobel Prizes: a bizarre juxtaposition if ever there was one. Available at: http://blogs.scientificamerican.com/the-curious-wavefunction/2012/11/20/chocolate-consumption-and-nobel-prizes-a-bizarre-juxta-position-if-there-ever-was-one/ (accessed 5 September 2014).

Kochanska, G. (2002) Committed compliance, moral self and internalization: a mediational model, *Developmental Psychology*, 38(3): 339–51.

Kochanska, G., Barry, R.A., Stellern, S.A. and O'Bleness, J.J. (2009) Early attachment organisation moderates the parent–child mutually coercive pathway to children's antisocial conduct, *Child Development*, 80(4): 1288–300.

Kochanska, G. and Sanghag ,K. (2013) Difficult temperament moderates links between maternal responsiveness and children's compliance and behaviour problems in low-income families, *Journal of Child Psychology and Psychiatry*, 54(3): 323–32.

Koestner, R. and Losier, G.F. (2002) Distinguishing three ways of being highly motivated: a closer look at introjection, identification and intrinsic motivation, in E.L. Deci and R.M. Ryan (eds) *The Handbook of Self-determination Research*. Rochester, NY: University of Rochester Press.

Krevans, J. and Gibbs, J.C. (1996) Parents' use of inductive discipline: relations to children's empathy and prosocial behaviour, *Child Development*, 67: 3263–77.

Kuczynski, L. and Kochanska, G. (1990) Development of children's noncompliance strategies, *Developmental Psychology*, 26(3): 398–408.

Lagattuta, K.H. and Wellman, H.M. (2001) Thinking about the past: early knowledge about links between prior experience, thinking and emotion, *Child Development*, 72: 82–102.

Lamb, M.E. (1978) Qualitative aspects of mother–infant and father–infant attachments in the second year of life, *Infant Behaviour and Development*, 1: 265–75.

Lamb, M.E. (2010) *The Role of the Father in Child Development*, 5th edn. Hoboken, NJ: Wiley.

Lepper, M., Greene, D. and Nisbett, R. (1973) Undermining children's intrinsic interest with extrinsic rewards: a test of the 'overjustification' hypothesis, *Journal of Personality and Social Psychology*, 28(1): 129–37.

Leslie, A.M. (1987) Pretense and representation: the origins of 'theory of mind', *Psychological Review*, 4: 412–26.

Licht, B., Simoni, H. and Perrig-Chiello, P. (2008) Conflict between peers in infancy and toddler age: what do they fight about? *Early Years: An International Research Journal*, 28(3): 235–49.

Lyons-Ruth, K. (1996) Attachment relationships among children with aggressive behaviour problems: the role of disorganized early attachment patterns, *Journal of Consulting and Clinical Psychology*, 64: 64–73.

Maccoby, E.M. (1980) *Social Development: Psychological Growth and the Parent–Child Relationship*. New York: Harcourt Brace Jovanovich.

MacLure, M., Jones, L., Holmes, R. and MacRae, C. (2012) Becoming a problem: behaviour and reputation in the early years classroom, *British Educational Research Journal*, 38: 447–71.

Main, M. (1996) Introduction to the special section on attachment and psychopathology: 2. overview of the field of attachment, *Journal of Consulting and Clinical Psychiatry*, 64(2): 237–43.

Main, M. and Hesse, E. (1990) Parents' unresolved traumatic experiences are related to infant disorganized attachment status: is frightened and/or frightening parental behavior the linking mechanism? in M.T. Greenberg, D. Cichetti and E.M. Cummings (eds) *Attachment in the Preschool Years: Theory, Research and Intervention*. Chicago: University of Chicago Press.

Main, M. and Solomon, J. (1990) Procedures for identifying infants as disorganized-disoriented during the Ainsworth Strange Situation, in M. Greenberg, D. Cicchetti and E.M. Cummings (eds) *Attachment in the Preschool Years: Theory, Research and Intervention*. Chicago: University of Chicago Press.

Martins, C. and Gaffan, E.A. (2000) Effects of maternal depression on patterns of infant–mother attachment: a meta-analytic investigation, *Journal of Child Psychology and Psychiatry*, 41(6): 737–46.

Maselko, J., Kubzansky, L., Lipsitt, L. and Buka, S.L. (2011) Mother's affection at 8 months predicts emotional distress in adulthood, *Journal of Epidemiology and Community Health*, 65(7): 621–5.

Maslow, A.H. (1943) A theory of human motivation, *Psychological Review*, 50(4): 370–93.

Mauss, I. (2005) Control your anger, *Scientific American Mind*, 16(4): 64–71.

Meins, E. (2014) Attachment, in A. Wenzel (ed.) *The Oxford Handbook of Perinatal Psychology*, Oxford Handbooks. Available at: www.oxfordhandbooks.com/view/10.1093/oxfordhb/9780199778072.001.0001/oxfordhb-9780199778072-e-005?rskey=TtNcDv&result=5 (accessed 20 September 2014).

Meins, E., Ferneyhough, C., de Rosnay, M. et al. (2012) Mind-mindedness as a multidimensional construct: appropriate and nonattuned mind-related comments independently predict infant–mother attachment in a socially diverse sample, *Infancy*, 17(4): 393–415.

Mischel, W., Shoda, Y. and Rodriguez, M.L. (1989) Delay of gratification in children, *Science*, 244(4907): 933–8.

Moffitt, T., Arseneault, L., Belsky, D. et al. (2011) A gradient of childhood self-control predicts health, wealth, and public safety, *PNAS, Proceedings of the National Academy of Sciences of the United States of America*, 108(7): 2693–8.

Montessori, M. (2005) *Dr. Montessori's Own Handbook*. Mineola, NY: Dover Publications. (Original work published in 1914).

Moullin, S., Waldfogel, J. and Washbrook, E. (2014) Baby bonds, parenting bonds: parenting, attachment and a secure base for children. Available at: http://www. suttontrust.com/wp-content/uploads/2014/03/baby-bonds-final.pdf (accessed 5 June 2014).

Mueller, C.M. and Dweck, C.S. (1998) Intelligence praise can undermine motivation and performance, *Journal of Personality and Social Psychology*, 75: 33–52.

Newland, L.A. and Coyl, D.D. (2010) Fathers' role as attachment figures: an interview with Sir Richard Bowlby, *Early Child Development and Care*, 180(1 & 2): 25–32.

Noble, T. and McGrath, H. (2013) Well-being and resilience in education, in L. Boniwell, S.A. David, and A.C. Ayers (eds) *The Oxford Book of Happiness*, Oxford Handbooks. Available at: http://www.oxfordhandbooks.com/view/10.1093/oxfordhb/9780199557257.001.0001/oxfordhb-9780199557257-e-043 (accessed 21 April 2014).

Nolen-Hoeksema, S., Wolfson, A., Mumme, D. and Gushkin, K. (1995) Helplessness in children of depressed and nondepressed mothers, *Developmental Psychology*, 31: 377–87.

Overmeier, J.B. and Seligman, M.E.P. (1967) Effects of inescapable shock upon subsequent escape and avoidance responding, *Journal of Comparative and Physiological Psychology*, 63: 28–33.

Parish-Morris, J., Golinkoff, R.M. and Hirsh-Pasek, K. (2013) From coo to code: a brief story of language development, in P.D. Zelazo (ed.) *The Oxford Handbook of Developmental Psychology*, vol. 1: *Body and Mind*, Oxford Handbooks. Available at: http://www.oxfordhandbooks.com/view/10.1093/oxfordhb/9780199958450.001.0001/oxfordhb-9780199958450-e-30?rskey=Abg7Rw&result=1 (accessed 31 October 2014).

Parker, G. (1983) *Parental Overprotection: A Risk Factor in Psychosocial Development.* New York: Grune and Stratton.

Paulssen-Hoogeboom, M.C., Stams, G.J., Hermanns, J.M., et al. (2008) Parenting style as a mediator between children's negative emotionality and problematic behaviour in early childhood, *Journal of Genetic Psychology*, 169(3): 209–26.

Porter, L. (2013) Applied behaviour analysis: its applications and limitations, in T. Cole, H. Daniels, and J. Visser (eds) *The Routledge International Companion to Emotional and Behavioural Difficulties.* London: Routledge.

Power, T.J., Blom-Hoffman, J., Clarke, A. et al .(2005) Reconceptualizing intervention integrity: a partnership-based framework for linking research with practice, *Psychology in the Schools*, 42(5): 495–507.

Reddy, V. (2008) *How Infants Know Minds.* London: Harvard University Press.

Ripley, K. and Yuill, N. (2005) Patterns of language impairment and behaviour in boys excluded from school, *British Journal of Educational Psychology*, 75(1): 37–50.

Roberts, J. and Donkin, A. with Pillas, P. (2014) *Measuring What Matters: A Guide for Children's Centres.* London: UCL Institute of Health Equity.

Rogers, C. (1961) *On Becoming a Person.* Boston: Houghton Mifflin.

Rose, J., Gilbert, L. and Smith, H. (2012) Emotion coaching, available at: http://www.attachmentawareschools.com/resources/documents/Emotion_Coaching_Pilot_Findings.pdf (accessed 7 September 2014).

Rosenthal, R. (2003) Covert communication in laboratories, classrooms and the truly real world, *Current Directions in Psychological Science*, 12(5): 151–4.

Rosenthal, R. and Jacobson, L. (1968) *Pygmalion in the Classroom: Teacher Expectation and Pupils' Intellectual Development.* New York: Holt, Rinehart and Winston.

Royer, E. (2013) Training and professional development for educators working with children and young people with EBD, in T. Coles, H. Daniels and J. Visser (eds) *The*

Routledge International Companion to Emotional and Behavioural Difficulties. London: Routledge.

Savina, E. (2014) Does play promote self-regulation in children? *Early Child Development and Care*, 184(11): 1692–705.

Schoon, I., Parsons, S., Rush, R. et al. (2010) Children's language ability and psychosocial development: a 29-year follow-up study, *Paediatrics*, 126: e73–e80.

Seligman, M.E.P. (2011) *Flourish. A New Understanding of Happiness and Well-Being and How to Achieve Them.* London: Nicholas Brealey Publishing.

Seligman, M.E.P. and Maier, S.F. (1967) Failure to escape traumatic shock, *Journal of Experimental Psychology*, 74: 1–9.

Siegel, A.E. and Kohn, L.G. (1959) Permissiveness, permission, and aggression: the effects of adult presence or absence on aggression in children's play, *Child Development*, 30: 131–41.

Singer, E. and de Haan, D. (2007) *The Social Lives of Young Children: Play, Conflict And Moral Learning in Day-Care Groups.* Amsterdam: SWP.

Skinner, E. and Edge, K. (2002) Self-determination, coping and development, in E.L Deci and R.M. Ryan (eds) *The Handbook of Self-determination Research.* Rochester, NY: University of Rochester Press.

Smith, C. (2003) *Writing and Developing Social Stories: Practical Interventions in Autism.* Milton Keynes: Speechmark Publishing.

Sorce, J.F., Emde, R.N., Campos, J. and Klinnart, M.D. (1985) Maternal emotional signalling: its effect on the visual cliff behaviour of 1-year-olds, *Developmental Psychiatry*, 21: 195–200.

Sroufe, L.A. (1990) Considering the normal and abnormal together: the essence of developmental psychopathology, *Development and Psychopathology*, 2: 335–47.

Sutton, C. (2012) Praises – five a day for young children, *The Psychologist*, 25(1): 32–5.

Sutton, J., Smith, P.K. and Swettenham, J. (1999) Bullying and theory of mind: a critique of the 'social skills deficit' view of anti-social behaviour, *Social Development*, 8(1): 117–27.

Thompson, R.A. (2013) Attachment theory and research: précis and prospect, in P.D. Zelazo (ed.) *The Oxford Handbook of Developmental Psychology*, vol. 2: *Self and Other*, Oxford Handbooks. Available at: http://www.oxfordhandbooks.com/view/10.1093/oxfordhb/9780199958474.001.0001/oxfordhb-9780199958474-e-009?rskey=3mhJOD&result=1#oxfordhb-9780199958474-div1-83 (accessed 20 September 2013).

Tominey, S.L.(2011) Red light, purple light: findings from a randomised trial using circle time games to improve behavioural self-regulation in preschool, *Early Education and Development*, 22: 489–519.

Tommerdahl, J. (2013) Links between emotional and behavioural difficulties and speech and language difficulties: what every teacher should know, in T. Coles, H. Daniels and J. Visser (eds) *The Routledge International Companion to Emotional and Behavioral Difficulties.* London: Routledge.

Tremblay, R.E., Nagin, D.S., Seguin, J.R. et al. (2004) Physical aggression during early childhood: trajectories and predictions, *Pediatrics*, 114(1): 3–9.

Tronick, E. (2007) *The Neurobehavioral and Social Emotional Development of Infants and Children.* New York: Norton.

UNICEF(1989) Convention on the Rights of the Child. Available at: http://www.unicef.org/crc/ (accessed 20 October 2014).

Van IJzendoorn, M.H., Schuengel, C. and Bakermans-Kranenberg, M.J. (1999) Disorganized attachment in early childhood: meta-analysis of precursors, concomitants, and sequelae, *Development and Psychopathology*, 11: 225–49.

Volling, B.L., MacKinnon Lewis, C., Rabiner, D., and Baradaran, L.P. (1993) Children's social competence and sociometric status: further exploration of aggression, social withdrawal, and peer rejection, *Development and Psychopathology*, 5: 459–83.

Vygotsky, L. (1978) *Mind in Society*. Cambridge MA: MIT Press. (Original work published in 1930.)

Webster-Stratton, C. and Taylor, T. (2001) Nipping early risk factors in the bud: preventing substance abuse, delinquency, and violence in adolescence through interventions targeted at young children (0–8 years), *Prevention Science*, 2(3): 165–92.

Webster-Stratton, C., Reinke, W.M., Herman, K.C. and Newcomer, L.L. (2011) The Incredible Years Teacher classroom management training: the methods and principles that support fidelity of training delivery, *School Psychology Review*, 40(4): 509–29.

Welsh, J.A., Nix, R.L., Blair, C. et al. (2010) The development of cognitive skills and gains in academic school readiness for children from low-income families, *Journal of Educational Psychology*, 102(1): 43–53.

Winnicott, D.W. (1965) *The Maturational Process and the Facilitative Environment*. New York: International Universities Press.

Winsler, A., Ducenne, L. and Koury, A. (2011) Singing one's way to self-regulation: the role of early music and movement curricula and private speech. *Early Education and Development*, 22: 274–304.

Index

harshness 49, 81, 87
having a go 40, 89–90, 98
healthy internalisation 3–9
healthy relatedness 16
helicopter parenting 51, 53
helping insecure attachments 35–45
heuristic play approach 95
hierarchy of needs 9–10
hijacking 62
Hooper, J. 9
hostility 38, 58
hot responses *see* emotions
how competence develops 91–102
humanist perspectives 6–7
Humphrey, N. 62–3
hyperactivity 138
hypervigilance 38

ignoring 72
imaginary play 18–19, 95–6, 118, 122
    see also pretend play
imitation 26, 33–4
importance of intrinsic motivation 93–6
importance of language 106
imprinting 22
incompetence 92
Incredible Years Teacher Classroom
    Management Training 136
inductive discipline 75–6, 107
inductive socialisation 75
infant-directed speech *see* 'motherese'
inflexibility 115–16
informational feedback 87
inhibition 32, 113–15, 118–19, 123
insecure attachment 35–45
    avoidant attachment 36–8
    in childcare settings 43–4
    disoriented attachment 40–41
    intervention 41–3
    resistant attachment 38–40
    'strange situation' 35–6
    using 'attachment lens' 44–5
intentional communication 110–111
interaction with others 116–23
internal representations 3–4, 98
internalising behaviour 2–3, 51, 88, 103–4
interpersonal experience 31
interpreting signals 33–4

interrupted activity 77–8
interventions to prevent insecure
    attachment 41–3
intimacy 67
intrinsic motivation 93–7
    accidental damage 96–7
intuition 65
irritability 43

jockey skills 112–13, 119, 123
    see also executive functions
Jogulekar, A. 7

key concepts of attachment theory 22–30
Key Person 19–23, 29–30, 37–41, 44, 57
Koestner, R. 48
Kopp, C.B. 53

labelling emotions 67
lack of aspiration 87–8
lack of control 92
lack of privacy 17–18
language skills *see* communication skills
language therapy 106
later-appearing emotions 64–8
leading activities 94–5
learning difference 121, 138
Lee, K. 119–20, 122
Leong, D.J. 117
Lepper, M. 96
Licht, B. 77–8
life events 23
lifespan model 11–12
listening empathically 67
longitudinal studies of attachment 7–8, 30
Lorenz, Konrad 22, 32–3
Losier, G.F. 48

Maccoby, E.M. 73–4
MacLure, M. 79
Main, Mary 36, 40
maintaining appropriate boundaries 56
Makaton signing 105, 111
making a difference 91–102
    contingent rewards 96–7
    controllable environment 91–3
    growth mindset 97–101
    intrinsic motivation 93–6

susceptibility to abuse 4
'Swinging Sixties' 56
symbolic understanding 95, 118
systems approach 28

tantrums 12, 71–3, 78, 126
Tavistock Clinic 21
theory of human motivation 9–10
theory of mind 75
theory-informed approach 6–9
thinking pauses 122
tools of the mind 117–18
transitional objects 29
trauma 23
Tronick, E. 26
'troubled families' 128
trust 26, 30, 37–8, 41
typical behaviour 3
typical development 71–3

UN Convention on the Rights of the Child 4
unconditional love 16
unconditional positive regard 98
undermining relatedness 17–18
understanding behavioural issues 1–13
    lifespan model 11–12
    nature vs. nurture 5
    needs-based approach 9–10
    positive approach to 2–4
    self-determination theory 10–11
    theory-informed approach 6–9
    valuing children's rights 4
understanding insecure attachments 35–45

understanding neurodevelopment 30–32
'unfinished baby' 33
uniqueness 70–83
    developing communication skills 78–80
    difference to support autonomy 73–8
    discovering difference 70–71
    self-determined autonomy 80–82
    typical development 71–3
United Nations Convention on the Rights of the Child 4
unmet needs 11–12
unreliability 36
use of feelings see emotions
using 'attachment lens' 44–5

value of secure attachment bond 20–34
valuing children's rights 4
verbal language 104, 123
visual cliff 26–7
visual cues 105–6, 111, 121, 123
Vygotsky, Lev 6, 94–5, 106, 116–18, 123

waiting see executive functions
wanting to be self see uniqueness
watchfulness 33–4
whispers of negative emotion 65
Winnicott, D.W. 26
wiring 31
working memory 19, 113, 118, 123
working together see collaboration

zone of proximal development 117
ZPD see zone of proximal development

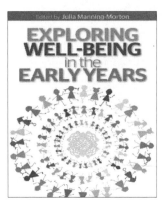

EXPLORING WELLBEING IN THE EARLY YEARS

Julia Manning-Morton

9780335246847 (Paperback)
October 2013

eBook also available

Children's experiences and well-being in their earliest years underpin and highly influence their future development and learning. Drawing on research with parents, children and a range of professionals in the early childhood field, this book considers how well-being is interpreted in the early childhood field. It includes snapshots of what our youngest children think about their well-being, and examines external environmental contexts that impact on well-being.

Key features:

- Focuses on appropriate pedagogical approaches and aspects of practice that support children's well-being
- Highlights the inseparability of adults' and children's well-being
- Prioritises children and families' socio-cultural contexts

www.openup.co.uk